LONDON TRANSFORMED

London Transformed

Images of the City in the Eighteenth Century

Max Byrd

New Haven and London   Yale University Press

1978

Copyright © 1978 by Yale University.
All rights reserved. This book may not be
reproduced, in whole or in part, in any form
(except by reviewers for the public press),
without written permission from the publishers.

Designed by John O. C. McCrillis
and set in Press Roman type.
Printed in the United States of America by
The Murray Printing Co., Westford, Massachusetts.

Published in Great Britain, Europe, Africa, and
Asia (except Japan) by Yale University Press,
Ltd., London. Distributed in Latin America by
Kaiman & Polon, Inc., New York City; in
Australia and New Zealand by Book & Film
Services, Artarmon, N.S.W., Australia; and in
Japan by Harper & Row, Publishers, Tokyo
Office.

Library of Congress Cataloging in Publication Data

Byrd, Max.
    London transformed.

Includes bibliographical references and index.
    1. English literature—18th century—History and
criticism. 2. London in literature. I. Title.
PR449.L65B95   820'.9'32   77-11875
ISBN 0-300-02166-6

For Walter Jackson Bate

Contents

Acknowledgments

I am deeply grateful to the National Endowment for the Humanities, which awarded me a Younger Humanist Fellowship for the academic year 1974–75 and thereby enabled me to begin writing. I am also grateful to the A. Whitney Griswold Fund of Yale University for an award in the same year, defraying the cost of a stay in London for research. The Faculty Research Fund of the University of California, Davis, and the Yale English Department absorbed the major expense of preparing the typescript. I am indebted to the Beinecke Library of Yale University, the British Library, the Members' Library of the London County Council, and the University of London Library for favors large and small. A few sentences in chapter 1 originally appeared in the introduction to my anthology, *Defoe: A Collection of Critical Essays* (Englewood Cliffs, N.J.: Prentice-Hall, 1975).

Many friends offered help, and I am especially grateful to Leo Braudy, Geoffrey Hartman, George deF. Lord, James C. Nohrnberg, and Martin Price for frequent kindnesses and much patience. To my students Lisa Schilit and Janet Howard I am indebted for several phrases and ideas. Alastair Goodlad, M.P., and Anne Riches were most thoughtful hosts in London. Ellen Graham of the Yale University Press demonstrated a consideration and an imperturbable good sense that still astonish me. And A. Bartlett Giamatti shared the worst coffee and the finest talk in the world for three splendid years.

In the midst of their own pressing work, W. B. Carnochan, Robert H. Hopkins, and George A. Starr all read a nearly final version and made invaluable corrections, annotations, and suggestions. Such generosity is like them, and it would be foolish not to show gratitude for their example as well as for their encouragement. This book had the great good luck, moreover, to be written two doors down the hall from

Michael G. Cooke, who improves everything he reads and whose friendship and criticism were equally inspiriting and sustaining. Brookes C. Byrd contributed materially to every page; her other gifts, of perspective, tolerance, and love, must go acknowledged but unrecorded here.

Finally, this book is dedicated to a scholar, teacher, and friend whose presence has been an inspiration to my generation of beginners. It is not enough to say that he has cleared my mind of a good deal of rubbish, true as that is, for he has also filled it with the indispensable premises of a moral education.

Introduction

How can one begin a book about eighteenth-century London
without Boswell's wonderful description?

> When we came upon Highgate hill and had a view of
> London, I was all life and joy. I repeated Cato's soliloquy
> on the immortality of the soul, and my soul bounded
> forth to a certain prospect of happy futurity. I sung all
> manner of songs, and began to make one about an amo-
> rous meeting with a pretty girl, the burthen of which was
> as follows:
>> She gave me *this*, I gave her *that*;
>> And tell me, had she not tit for tat?
> I gave three huzzas, and we went briskly in.[1]

He was just twenty-two when he arrived at Highgate Hill, and
we are not likely to confuse his urbanity with that of Lord
Chesterfield, say, or Horace Walpole. "Maybe there never was
anyone as young as Boswell was in the spring of 1763," as
Christopher Morley says. But if he fails to dazzle us with his
polish, if his noisy greeting would echo strangely in the
drawing rooms of Hanover Square, Boswell expresses per-
fectly another sort of urbanity: that exuberant and powerful
attraction toward London that the moth knows for the
candle and that every English generation since the Renaissance
has deeply, irresistibly felt. Part of its attraction belongs to
all great cities, of course, and radiates from New York or
Paris or Rome as well as London. Yet another part of its
allure must remain forever guesswork, in which subjective
speculation such as V. S. Pritchett has recently written, or
lyrical outbursts like the sixteenth-century poet William
Dunbar's for his new home, will come nearer the fact than
any scholarship:

1

London, thou art of Townes A per se.
Soveraign of Cities, semeliest in sight,
Of high Renoun, Riches and Royaltie;
Of Lordes, Barons and many goodly knyght,
Of most delectable lusty ladies bright;
Of famous prelates in habites clericall;
Of merchauntes full of substance and of myght,
London, thou art the flour of Cities all.[2]

But to later generations, and not simply of Englishmen, this spell arises also in good measure from the special place London held in eighteenth-century life.

The city that Boswell saluted with three brisk huzzas was by far the largest in Europe, a third again as large as Paris, containing one-tenth the population of England, the great, glittering capital of a country beginning to assume, with perfect confidence, an empire. It dominates English consciousness in the eighteenth century as, to use a favorite analogy of the time, the head dominates the body. When Boswell's soul bounded outward into happy futurity, London had not yet become Cobbett's great wen nor had its furnaces and factories yet become satanic mills. In the smoky warrens to the east and south of the City, it is true, poverty festered and the despoiling architecture of modern commerce spread like gray rot; in another two generations, awareness of London's miserable underworld would have become virtually general, movements for reform and philanthropy become Victorian institutions. The prospect that ran southward from Highgate Hill, however, presented to Boswell's eyes, not the first columns of Industrial Revolution, but rather a panorama of steeples rising like stalks above an endless plain of brick and slate and wood, weaving together toward the river. To Boswell's left St. Paul's Cathedral its dusky dome upheaved, Wren's one successful, magnificent effort to pour the Augustan city into a Renaissance mold. To his right sparkled Pall Mall, St. James's Park, the new bridge at Westminster, and the great Abbey itself. Before him Bloomsbury, where the lords Bedford and Montague had placed their mansions along Great Russell Street, between Covent Garden and the green countryside of Islington.

Eighteenth-century London usually calls to mind irresistible Hogarthian images of vitality like these. Simply to name
its streets and places is a special pleasure, and evokes an atmosphere of social confidence, of appetite and passion, of
vigorous civility; when we think of it, we think of an age
celebrated for the arts of living, and we recreate in our imaginations the haunts of Boswell and Johnson, the Fountain
tavern, the theater of Garrick and Peg Woffington, the sinu-
ous machinations of Robert Walpole.

But it will not do to sound too much like Thackeray pining
for the vanished reign of Queen Anne. There is a second reason, apart from the splendid energy of its life, why that London still interests us. The city that Boswell embraces like a
pretty girl also contained a squalor, a hopelessness, that we
cannot easily imagine today; and while to the literary critic
those things most often seem no more than a sad, noisy, and
inevitable background for greater doings, to the historian
they point forward to a new chapter in urban history. London's extraordinary growth during the period 1700–1820, its
wealth, its cultural achievements and massive humane failings
all foreshadow the changes—economic, political, social—that
were to come over European and American cities in the nineteenth century but that were already under way in England
in the eighteenth. In accounts more sober than Boswell's,
the tensions between growth and mastery become increasingly
apparent and explain in part so many references to the city as
somehow a living being, the fascination so many writers feel
for its slightest shiftings, its minute adjustments of weight
and pressure: as if they watch a great, dangerous creature stir
in its slumber.

These are unique historical conditions, however. We concern ourselves with the character of eighteenth-century
London now, not chiefly for its lessons in civic history and
management, but because its greatest writers found in it a
timeless moral image. Pope, Swift, Johnson, Reynolds, Burke:
I am thinking of the group Paul Fussell has called the Augustan Humanists.[3] Their dream, inherited from the classical
world, was of an ordered community gathered into the form
of a beautiful city like Rome or Athens: an image of harmony

and transcendence to be placed against the equally classical form of a city of vice, like the Babylon of Revelation, and also against the chafing daily realities of life in London. Our dream, inherited from them, breaks no less regularly against such disappointments; but if we have been lucky, we have likewise inherited their courage to see at once both ideal and fact, and to abandon neither.

This study had its beginnings in my earlier book, *Visits to Bedlam: Madness and Literature in the Eighteenth Century* (University of South Carolina Press, 1974). There I discussed briefly the later eighteenth-century tendency to describe London with the metaphor of a gigantic Bedlam and to blame the most troubling stresses of modern life upon the inadequacies of the city. My purpose here, however, is not to write the history of London or to offer yet another sketch of eighteenth-century social life—tempting though it is to think of adding a few pages more to the literature on such items as the earl of Salisbury's hobby of driving stagecoaches through the streets; Burridge the Blasphemer, so notorious for profanity that newspapers printed his name in Gothic type; the Chelsea Water Works; the architecture of Covent Garden; the eighteenth-century custom of holding funerals at night; the interesting juxtaposition of the Houses of Parliament and Thieves Lane (now nonexistent); the toyshop in Charing Cross, near Hogarth's house. But that work has already been done by many abler hands. My interest instead is in tracing several recurrent images of London at key points in the century, images that appear in every century and for every city, but that are charged with unusual interest here. What I see taking place as London grows larger and larger, more and more unmanageable, is paradoxically an increasing effort to humanize the city, to bring it to terms with the human scale of imagination, to force what is beyond comprehension back into traditional forms of comprehension. Cities are after all the largest of man-made things. As the size and complexity of London reach past the boundaries of humanist understanding, the humanist imagination reworks those boundaries and sometimes, as in the case of Blake, transcends them altogether.

I begin and end with the city under threat of annihilation and with the image of the human body. Defoe and Blake, like all of us, faced with the spectacle of London, resort to the oldest possible measurement for comparison: they reduce the unthinkable proportions of the city to the plausible ones of faces and arms and legs. The impulse to measure the outward world by ourselves begins with infancy and lasts through life—its presence in Renaissance thought has been authoritatively studied by Leonard Barkan in *Nature's Work of Art*[4]—and we are likely to come upon it anywhere and everywhere in our reading: in the moving passage in *Civilization and Its Discontents,* for example, where Freud compares the psyche to the ancient city of Rome in which each archaeological level has been built upon another—"an entity, that is to say, in which nothing that has once come into existence will have passed away and all the earlier phases of development continue to exist alongside the latest one."[5] Or we may encounter it in Walter Shandy's criticism of the enormous size of London: "a *distemper* was here his favourite metaphor, and he would run it down into a perfect allegory, by maintaining it was identically the same in the body national as in the body natural, where blood and spirits were driven up into the head faster than they could find their ways down;—a stoppage of circulation must ensue, which was death in both cases."[6] In *A Journal of the Plague Year,* Defoe presents London as a body torn by fever, a body diseased, plague-ridden, and misshapen; and in the intensity of his response, his special vision of London carries it to the edge of the grave. Blake, if anything more intense, turns in the opposite direction and offers us the picture of Jerusalem, a woman who is also London and whose beautiful body is its transcendent form.

Between these two apocalyptic visions I trace those less spectacular but no less necessary images that such writers as Pope, Johnson, and Wordsworth use over and over to picture London: images of theaters, rivers, language—images that appear also in Defoe and Blake and dozens of other writers. These metaphors—my list is not meant to be exhaustive—occur in discussions of other cities than London and in other times. They belong, indeed, to a permanent repository of figures for our attempts to civilize ourselves. If we want to discover the particularities of eighteenth-century London's appearance or the details of its growth, there are both contemporary and scholarly guides to consult. If we want to discover the *feel* of London life—its crowds and smells and sounds—there are still more immediate sources:

> We mov'd on till we came to *Fleet-bridge,* where *Nuts, Ginger-bread, Oranges* and *Oysters,* lay pil'd up in Moveable Shops that Run upon Wheeles, attended by Ill-looking Fellows, some with but one Eye, and others without Noses. Over-against these stood a parcel of *Trugmoldei's,* in Straw-Hats and Flat-Caps, selling Socks and Furmity, Night-Caps and Plumb-Pudding. Just as we pass'd by, a Feud was kindling between two Rival Females, who from the Brimstone of *Lust,* had blown up such a Fire of *Jealousie* between 'em, that one call'd the other Adulterous Bitch; and Then falling into Tears, express'd herself further in these Words, *Have I lent you the Money out of my Pocket, the Gown off my Back, and my Petticoat off my Arse, to be thus ungratefully rewarded? You know, Hussie, I have given you the very Bread out of my Mouth; but before you shall take my Bed-fellow from my Belly, you Whore, I'll Tare your Eyes out;* and then, with Teeth and Nails, made a Violent assault upon her Rival, who roar'd out for help, and crying out she was Quick with Child, the Mobb hearing her plead her Belly, were mov'd to Compassion, and so part'd 'em, their Coifs having receiv'd the greatest Dammage in the fray.[7]

But if we want to discover the enduring moral patterns behind this life, we must turn to an entirely different kind of writer.

"The humanist instinct looks in the world for physical conditions that are related to our own," writes Geoffrey Scott in *The Architecture of Humanism,*

> for movements which are like those we enjoy, for resistances that resemble those that can support us, for a

setting where we should be neither lost nor thwarted. It looks, therefore, for certain masses, lines, and spaces, tends to create them and recognizes their fitness when created. And, by our instinctive imitation of what we see, their seeming fitness becomes our real delight.

But besides these favourable physical states, our instinct craves for order, since order is the pattern of the human mind. And the pattern of the mind, no less than the body's humour, may be reflected in the concrete world. Order in architecture means the presence of fixed relations in the position, the character and the magnitude of its parts. It enables us to interpret what we see with greater readiness; it renders form intelligible by making it coherent; it satisfies the desires of the mind; it humanises architecture.[8]

These sentences contain the heart of my explorations: the humanizing of London, which is carried out by imaging it as a human body, as human language, as human art. What the eighteenth-century experience of these images can show us, apart from the inherent fascination of London itself, is what its greatest writers always show us: the struggle of human beings to control the energies that bring them together, to civilize themselves; the struggle to maintain a balance between our need to fashion an individual work (of art, of life) and that other need to share what we have built without destroying it. The heavenly city that Socrates describes to Glaucon near the end of *The Republic* is our earliest instance of a complex of ideas widespread enough in Western culture to be called an archetype: it is the virtuous community whose gates all men hope in time to enter. Real cities, earthly and imperfect, underlie and shape that vision, ones like Troy, Athens, Rome, Jerusalem, and London. But as Socrates warned and as the Augustan humanists understood, the cities without are built upon the cities within, and their separate moral orders are continuous and alike.

1

Defoe's London:
"this prodigious Thing"

At Hampton Court in the late spring of 1722, not many miles from the village of Twickenham where three years earlier Alexander Pope had settled, Daniel Defoe paused in his *Tour thro' the Whole Island of Great Britain* to describe the prospect of the Thames as it stretches eastward toward London. Amid "the Beauty of the Country, the pleasant Situations, the Glory of innumerable fine Buildings, Noblemens and Gentlemens Houses, and Citizens Retreats" runs the river:

> high enough to be navigable, and low enough to be a little pleasantly rapid; so that the Stream looks always cheerful, not slow and sleeping, like a Pond. This keeps the Waters always clear and clean, the Bottom in view, the Fish playing, and in sight; and in a Word, it has every Thing that can make an Inland; or, as I may call it, a Country River, pleasant and agreable. [I, 173] [1]

Then in a burst of good-natured bluffness he goes on to explain what we must and must not expect from a simple journalist like himself:

> I shall sing you no Songs here of the River in the first Person of a Water Nymph, a Goddess, (and I know not what) according to the Humour of the ancient Poets. I shall talk nothing of the Marriage of old *Isis,* the Male River, with the beautiful *Thame,* the Female River, a Whimsy as

simple as the Subject was empty, but I shall speak of the
River as Occasion presents, as it really is *made glorious* by
the Splendor of its Shores, gilded with noble Palaces,
strong Fortifications, large Hospitals, and publick Buildings; with the greatest Bridge, and the greatest City in the
World, made famous by the Opulence of its Merchants, the
Encrease and Extensiveness of its Commerce; by its invincible Navies, and by the innumerable Fleets of Ships
sailing upon it, to and from all Parts of the World.

As I meet with the River upwards in my Travels thro'
the Inland Country, I shall speak of it as it is the Chanel
for conveying an infinite Quantity of Provisions from remote Counties to *London,* and enriching all the Counties
again that lye near it, by the return of Wealth and Trade
from the City; and in describing these Things I expect
both to inform and divert my Readers, and speak, in a
more Masculine Manner, more to the Dignity of the Subject, and also more to their Satisfaction, than I could do
any other way. [I, 173–74]

He may have had in mind as he wrote just such a "Whimsy"
as Pope nearby had spun about the Thames and its city in
Windsor-Forest, a gorgeous vision of river gods, "glitt'ring
Spires," and streams of silver. Or he may have been simply recalling the long English folk tradition of animating this particular kind of setting. It is clear in any case that he means to
set himself in opposition to tradition, to turn his back on
false reporting and to lay before his readers the scene as it
really is. It is clear also that what draws his eye is the vast
metropolis that sprawls along the horizon, the "greatest City
in the World," the perpetual focus of his whole extended,
ambitious survey. And though writers at least as prosaic as
Defoe, stirred by the subject, had cleared their throats to
celebrate it, even here he intends to maintain his masculine
factualness. London no more than the Thames takes its fame
from empty fantasy or ancient humors; to speak of the city
as it too "really is *made glorious,*" Defoe at once begins to
name the "Opulence of its Merchants" and the "Encrease and
Extensiveness of its Commerce."

I

At the center of Defoe's vision of London lies the market-place. It appears everywhere in his accounts of the city, explicitly in the concerns of his journalism and the action of his novels, implicitly in the images of trade that surface continually like bubbles in his prose: stock exchanges, merchants, stores, credit, profit and loss. And everywhere he would have us believe that his vision is realistic, reliable, factual, that he has replaced the ambiguous figures of poetical writers with the useful, unequivocal figures of business; he flattens his style (if he cannot be said to smooth it) and scrapes away deliberately those secondary meanings that the spectacle of a great city ordinarily excites in us. The nebulous glimmerings of a holy city or an ideal city are banished; his clear-sighted perspective exposes only the "Wealth and Trade" and "Things" of London. Even in *A Journal of the Plague Year,* when the city has come to its knees under the impact of an inexplicable disaster, the usual meaning of London for Defoe continues to assert itself: a marketplace first, and only incidentally thereafter a place for other human needs and aspirations:

> *John* argu'd very calmly with them a great while, and told them, "That *London* was the Place by which they, that is, the Townsmen of *Epping* and all the Country round them, subsisted; to whom they sold the produce of their Lands, and out of whom they made the Rent of their Farms; and to be so cruel to the Inhabitants of *London,* or to any of those by whom they gain'd so much was very hard, . . . when they fled from the Face of the most terrible Enemy in the World; that it would be enough to make the Name of an *Epping*-Man hateful thro' all the City, and to have the Rabble Stone them in the very Streets, whenever they came so much as to Market." [142][2]

Defoe's claim to literal accuracy, persuasive enough as one turns the two fat volumes of the *Tour,* is just what we should expect of him. Reared in a Dissenting household and suspicious of every fiction, he took constant, almost obsessive pains to establish the truthfulness of what he wrote. Even the novels for which he is now chiefly remembered—*Robinson Crusoe, Moll Flanders, Roxana*—are introduced as genuine autobiographies; and almost all of his works, novels and journalism alike, are lumpy with catalogues, inventories, tables, and lists: stockpiles for a plain style. He spoke, after all, for a new generation of exacting, straightforward businessmen. His audience in *The Complete English Tradesman, The Review, A General History of Trade,* and a hundred other hasty essays and pamphlets was precisely the merchant middle class that had been cast into political and social ascendancy by the wars of the seventeenth century, a class indifferent to the classical, aristocratic literature of earlier periods, indeed by education excluded from it. For them a picture of London much like Defoe's had long been in the making: careful descriptions of streets, buildings, and curiosities had been accumulating steadily since John Stow had issued his monumental *Survey* in 1598; and that Survey itself had recently been brought up to date and reprinted by John Strype in a series of editions beginning in 1720. Other writers, notably John Macky in his pedestrian *Journey through England* (1714), had literally covered the same ground, as had the anonymous authors of a growing number of guidebooks for visitors.

It would have been remarkable, however, if Defoe had succeeded in flattening entirely the ancient background of allusion and meaning against which others might see his city. Palaces, domes, fortifications, magnificent public buildings, for example, with all their symbolic suggestiveness enter inevitably into any description of a city, old style or new. Or again, when Defoe organizes the prospect of London into city and river, in the *Tour* and frequently elsewhere, he reminds us necessarily of a traditional usage; his caution that we may expect no mythology of river nymphs and goddesses from him, truthful as it is, only slightly disguises that other mythical vision he immediately invokes with "the greatest Bridge, and the greatest City in the World." He sounds in fact a classical resonance in most readers' minds, for the associa-

tion of city and river reaches back in Western literature to
Homer and his picture in the *Iliad* of the doomed city of
Troy, riding fatefully above the plain where the Simois meets
the Skamandros. Rome, with which Defoe like all eighteenth-
century writers often compares London, closes around the
river Tiber, whose name is virtually synonymous with the
city. Babylon and the Tigris, Paris and the Seine, Cairo and
the Nile—the list stretches backward and forward across time
and space; and outside history even the most hardheaded of
Defoe's businessmen would remember that through the New
Jerusalem of John's Revelation flows "a pure river of water
of life, clear as crystal," fertilizing the gardens of life on
either side and forming a figurative street in the city. Explanations for this familiar association can be drawn from
many sources—from the twentieth century's arsenal of arche-
types, from the realities of commercial geography, from our
simple need to offset what is hard and artificial with what is
fluid and natural—but the effect is the same, to establish un-
avoidable points of reference and continuity.

What is striking nonetheless in Defoe's portraits of London
is the extent to which he actually does eliminate such possibilities for reference and meaning. Confronted in the *Tour*
with "a fair Prospect of the whole City of *London* it self"—
an invitation to metaphor on a grand scale—he allows himself
comparisons if not actual metaphors: "the most glorious
Sight without exception, that the whole World at present can
show, or perhaps ever cou'd since the Sacking of *Rome* in the
European and the burning of the Temple of *Jerusalem* in the
Asian part of the World" (I, 168). But when he begins his
proper description of London, these extravagances are mas-
sively counterbalanced by page after page of detail and cal-
culation, an account so relentlessly factual that, just as he
warned us, it has apparently nothing at all in common with
those ornate, allegorical commemorations that English writers
since Dunbar and Spenser had created for London, much less
with those visionary cities of Plato, John, and Augustine.
Perhaps as a consequence Defoe's London, here and in the
novels, always emerges as curiously featureless, as a collection

of names—of streets, buildings, squares—but not as a realized picture. One can trace Moll Flanders's movements, for example, accurately on a map; yet the London she moves through remains somehow two-dimensional, an abstract environment, so to speak, without colors or smells or windows and doors: the vividness we remember springs from Moll's own vigorous personality, not from any Hogarthian rendering of the tactile, visual life around her.

> I went thro' into *Bartholomew Close*, and then turn'd round to another Passage that goes into *Long-lane*, so away into *Charterhouse-Yard* and out into *St. John's-street*, then crossing into *Smithfield*, went down *Chick-lane* and into *Field-lane* to *Holbourn-bridge*, when mixing with the Crowd of People usually passing there, it was not possible to have been found out. [194] [3]

The names and movements together create a pattern of action rather than a setting, so that in the end London exists for us only as a network of traffic, a gigantic system for comings and goings, for transactions: what Auden somewhere calls an "abstract civic space."

Only in a second familiar classical motif does Defoe generate the kind of emotion about his subject that ultimately betrays him into complex, unfactual meaning. In the section of the *Tour* given over entirely to London, Letter V, he begins by exclaiming at the enormity of his task, more precisely, at the enormity of London. The ancient city has long ago overrun its own walls and spilled out in every direction, "New Squares, and new Streets rising up every Day to such a Prodigy of Buildings, that nothing in the World does, or ever did, equal it, except old *Rome* in *Trajan*'s Time, when the Walls were Fifty Miles in Compass, and the Number of Inhabitants Six Millions Eight hundred thousand Souls" (I, 316). [4] The sheer size of London staggers Defoe; and to come to terms with its immensity, to comprehend what has passed comprehension, he resorts to the timeless metaphor of the human body:

> It is the Disaster of *London*, as to the Beauty of its Fig-

ure, that it is thus stretched out in Buildings, just at the
Pleasure of every Builder, or Undertaker of Buildings,
and as the Convenience of the People directs, whether
for Trade, or otherwise; and this has spread the Face of
it in a most straggling, confus'd Manner, out of all Shape,
uncompact, and unequal; neither long or broad, round or
square; whereas the City of *Rome,* though a Monster for
its greatness, yet was, in a manner, round, with very few
Irregularities in its Shape.

The contrast with Trajan's Rome, which somehow maintained
its symmetry despite the pressure of "Six Millions," only
serves to emphasize the unclassical energy of modern London, a city that appears to "spread" and stretch like an independent being. And yet Defoe struggles (as any of us would)
to organize the city, to discover in his mind if nowhere else
a shape for it: thus the "Beauty of its Figure," a tentative ab-
straction, quickly focuses into "the Face of it" (while Rome
is in part a "Monster"). In the two pages that follow Defoe
turns again and again to images of the human body for his
description—"Newington reaches out her Hand *North,*"
"Westminster is in a fair Way to shake Hands with *Chelsea,*
as St. *Gyles*'s is with *Marybone.*" "All this is very evident,"
he says of London's immediate future, sounding for all the
world like a Lilliputian contemplating Gulliver, "and yet all
these put together, are still to be called *London:* Whither will
this monstrous City then extend?" As a temporary stay, he
has "caused a Measure to be taken of this mighty, I cannot
say uniform, Body."

These intimations of metaphor, scattered and indistinct
enough in themselves, belong to a perennial habit of mind.
To compare a city (or the political state it stands for) to the
proportions and parts of a human body has been commonplace since Plato, as we have already seen, and the eighteenth
century is a magazine of examples. Bernard Mandeville, like
Defoe a rather willfully accurate writer, opens *The Fable of
the Bees* with an analogy between London and the human
body; an anonymous pamphleteer in 1747 turns easily to the
same image to express a familiar fear:

And then, to behold the prodigious Growth and Increase of this unwieldy City, and to observe what a strange Multitude of People there is jumbled together in it? Who can reflect upon this, but must necessarily believe, that the Head in a little Time longer will grow so much too big for the Body, that it must consequently tumble down at last, and ruin the Whole?[5]

Josiah Tucker repeats it in 1783 and anticipates William Cobbett's famous phrase:

London, the Metropolis of *Great-Britain,* has been complained of, for Ages past, as a kind of Monster, with a Head enormously large, and out of all Proportion to its Body. And yet at that Juncture, when this Complaint was first made (about 200 Years ago) The Buildings of *London* were hardly advanced beyond the City-Bounds: As to *Westminster* and *Southwark* (which we now consider as united to the former by their Buildings and Bridges, and making on the whole, a City of a most immense Size) they were then little better than large straggling Villages. If therefore the Increase of Building, begun at such an early Period, was looked upon to be no better than a Wen, or Excrescence, in the Body Politic, what must we think of those numberless Streets and Squares, which have been added since!—For my Part, I do not think those Protuberances arose to any very alarming magnitude 'till within these 60 or 70 Years.[6]

Defoe himself uses variations of the comparison often outside the *Tour:* "'Tis impossible to enumerate the Particulars of the Damage suffered," he writes of the famous storm of 1703, "and of the Accidents which happened under these several Heads, in and about the City of *London:* The Houses looked like Skeletons, and an universal Air of Horror seem'd to sit on the Countenances of the People."[7] Or frequently: "The circulation of trade within our selves, where all the several manufactures move in a just rotation from the several countries where they are made, to the city of *London,* as the blood in the body to the Heart. . . ."[8] In this image, however, as in the image of city and river, Defoe seems to raze the elaborate system of correspondences that earlier writers had constructed. The sixteenth-century author of "A Discourse of London," for example, pursues the image far beyond commerce into widening circles of relationships:

> At once, Propagation of the Religion, the Execution of good Policy, the Exercise of Charity, and the Defence of the Country, is best performed by Towns and Cities. And this Civil Life approacheth nearest to the Shape of that mystical Body whereof Christ is the Head, and Men be the Members. Whereupon, both, at the first, that Man of God, *Moses,* in the Commonwealth of the *Israelites,* and the Governors of all Countries, in all Ages sithence, have continually maintained the same. And to change it, were nothing else but to metamorphose the World, and to make wild Beasts of reasonable Men.[9]

And toward the end of *Areopagitica,* in one of the best-known similes of seventeenth-century prose, Milton moves in beautiful complication from an image of the builders of a temple to "spiritual architecture," to London besieged, to a figure of the human body in good health and cheerfulness, and finally to "a noble and puissant nation rousing herself like a strong man after sleep, and shaking her invincible locks."[10]

Beside such instances Defoe's versions may come to seem unduly simple, shrunken. His London has no correlation with the mystical body of Christ, or with spiritual architecture and the harmoniously proportioned body of truth: it takes form before us instead as the head upon a distorted body, a misshapen giant, a monster whose astounding size is superficially a source of pride, but more deeply a source of terror. And we may remember, as we try to account for the vague unease his description in the *Tour* causes, that giants are variously interpreted by symbolists as the collective identity of a people— Blake's Albion, for example—or as some powerful unconscious element in each of us, like the libido or the archetypal father figure; but every reader of fairy tales knows that they also always represent a threatening, potentially destructive force never fully under control, one that must be placated or outwitted or killed. Defoe's sense of London as restless, unpredictable, devouring awakens a universal anxiety: we can hardly wonder that so much of Letter V is given over to attempts to fence in the city, to erect a "Circumvallation."

II

When we look closely at the image of the marketplace we see the same anxiety. The influential criticism of Mark Schorer and Ian Watt has helped us to understand the extent of Defoe's preoccupation with commerce—and perhaps to be a little scornful of it—but readers are sometimes not fully alert to the nervousness Defoe expresses about a life of business.[11] For it often appears that especially in his fiction the marketplace, to vary the image, is a theater for gentility. There his characters act out capitalism's reassuring drama of labor and reward, the conclusion of which is an undramatic bourgeois gentility; getting and spending they lay up their powers. Defoe's writings are saturated with scenes of tradesmen at work, with the handling of goods, with snatches of dialogue between customers and shopkeepers. And London's chief role is to make possible this satisfying prosperity: *"London* consumes all, circulates all, exports all, and at last pays for all, and this greatness and wealth of the City is the Soul of the Commerce to all the Nation; and as there is the greatest number of Tradesmen in this City, that are to be seen in any Place in the World; so they again support, and supply an innumerable number of Shopkeepers and Tradesmen of every kind in the Country, and in every part of the Country."[12] Defoe even raises the idea to the level of principle in a pamphlet called *Giving Alms No Charity* (1704), where a discussion of Flanders leads him to an optimistic recital of the domino effect, maintaining that "Multitudes of People make Trade, Trade makes Wealth, Wealth builds Cities, Cities enrich the Land round them, Land Enrich'd rises in Value, and the Value of Lands Enriches the Government."[13] But the marketplace is by no means a reliable mechanism for all these purposes: boom and bust are the tracks of its cycle, not a steady progression of "enrichings." And when the market falters—when a merchant's commodity fails to sell, for example, as Moll Flanders's beauty eventually does—confidence dissolves, values plunge; its victims literally panic. Colonel Jack's hysteria over the loss of his gold is a famous case, but even a sober handbook like *The Complete English Tradesman* is shot through with forebodings of bankruptcy, failure, collapse.[14] The great emotion that Defoe portrays, Benjamin Boyce has argued, rescuing him from the charge of arid verisimilitude, is fear—fear of God, fear of poverty, fear of uncertainty.[15] It is no surprising emotion to find in someone who entered Newgate prison seven times in his life, four times for political offenses, three times for debt; or in someone who twice was bankrupt. But it would be no less surprising if these anxieties did not in some way tarnish the splendor of London, that soul and heart of English commerce, that "grand Emporium of the Universe," as one contemporary called it.[16]

We may discover signs of strain, to take a convenient example, in Defoe's picture of the Royal Exchange in Cornhill, which served any number of eighteenth-century writers as a miniature of commercial London. While a Voltaire or an Addison thought of it as a miracle of harmony—a secular temple where "le Juif, le Mahométan et le Chrétien traitent l'un avec l'autre comme s'ils étaient de la même Religion, et ne donnent le nom d'infidèles qu'à ceux qui font banqueroute"—Defoe's representation is more ominous, less complacently good-humored.[17] In the *Tour* the Exchange draws predictable superlatives, "the greatest and finest of the Kind in the World," though its business has fallen off inauspiciously of late, and some shops in its arcade are left empty. But in *Colonel Jack* we feel a more palpable tension: in the midst of the Long Room of the Custom House, a hectic market, Jack commits his first crime, the theft of a packet of bank notes; and from there progresses to haunt the doors of the Exchange itself, milling with the crowd and stealing recklessly from the pockets of distracted brokers. Moll Flanders, more genteel in appearance, does not hesitate to enter the New

Exchange on the Strand, a similar building of shops and galleries: "I WENT off from the Shop, as if driven along by the Throng, and mingling myself with the Crowd, went out at the other Door of the *Exchange,* and so got away before they miss'd their Lace" (256–57).

The recurrent conjunction of business and crime in Defoe's fiction is suggestive—and we would not go too far, I think, if we saw Moll's and Jack's thefts as mirroring the unscrupulous practices of the legitimate Exchange. Indeed, other eighteenth-century writers had already begun to make plain the implications: the urban marketplace is as well adapted to crime as to commerce; Moll can steal as well as sell. In 1705 Bernard Mandeville scandalized England with a poem called *The Grumbling Hive* (later reworked as *The Fable of the Bees; or, Private Vices, Public Benefits*), a homely parable in which the mutual dependence of prosperity and vice was bluntly stated. And John Gay had pointed out the correlation in another way through his reversal of great world and underworld, first in an unacted farce, *The Mohocks* (1712), and afterward in *The Beggar's Opera* (1728). Defoe offers no such witty equation of virtue and vice as Mandeville and Gay provide, however. Reluctantly he recognizes the Mandevillean paradox that "Trade," as he admits in *The Complete English Tradesman,* "is almost universally founded upon Crime," yet he prefers to compartmentalize its terms and to keep them rigidly separate in his work.[18] There is a note of slack-jawed amazement, in fact, in his description of the effrontery of Jonathan Wild, the notorious receiver of stolen goods, who "openly kept his Compting House, or Office, like a Man of Business, and had his Books to enter every thing in with the utmost Exactness and Regularity."[19] But readers of *Moll Flanders* and *Roxana* will hardly be surprised to see these businesslike techniques oiling the operations of crime. Defoe well understands how the love of profit or the love of luxury seduces even the most upright tradesman to fraudulent dealings; more sharply still, he understands how poverty or sheer survival incites a man to crime: "How many honest gentlemen have we in England," he asks in the *Review,* "of

good Estates and noble circumstances, that would be High-
way Men, and come to the Gallows, if they were poor?"[20]
Morally and consciously he condemns the confusion of crime
and commerce; but sometimes in his imagination they undeniably merge, and mimic and feed each other, just as they
do at the Exchange, staining and corrupting the social order.

III

The London that sustains England's trade necessarily partakes of this ambiguity. Its wickedness grows almost in proportion to its prosperity. The grand emporium sparkling so
impressively downstream from Hampton Court becomes on
closer view a darkened wilderness where citizens move warily
past each other, distrustful of appearances, fearful of violence,
stupefied with vice. The city trades chiefly in luxury and
excess, as Defoe laments in a long chapter of *The Complete
English Tradesman;* its prosperity is dearly bought. Compared
to barbaric Constantinople, London is found to be so great a
metropolis only because it nurtures alehouses, chophouses,
gin shops, footmen, coachmen, pimps, and every kind of self-
indulgence. The Londoner defies all sumptuary laws, all
moderation, all restraints upon his pleasure. "What a poor
Nation must we have been," he asks (not without pride), "if
we had been a sober, religious, temperate Nation?" (II, ii,
106). Defoe's great, perplexed theme of London as marketplace, in short, opens his way toward the secondary theme of
London as a sink of corruption. The city's tinsel luxury does
not disguise the moral cost. "*London,* that us'd to be the
most safe and peaceful City in the Universe," he complains in
Augusta Triumphans (1728), "is now a Scene of Rapine and
Danger"; and tirelessly he proposes reforms to wipe the city
clean of gambling, whorehouses, private madhouses, drunkenness, and robbery.[21] The very squalor of the streets dismays
him, the clamor and the filth; in another pamphlet he dwells
on the hopeless existence of London urchins: "'Tis scarce
credible what a black Throng they are," he writes; "many of
them indeed perish young, and dye miserable, before they
may be said to look into Life; some are starv'd with Hunger,
some with Cold, many are found frozen in the Streets and

Fields, some drowned before they are old enough to be hang'd."[22] And *Due Preparations for the Plague* reverses his perspective on the river in the *Tour* with a long, disgusted account of the Thames-side along Wapping and Redrift Wall, an area of tidal pools, hogyards, and crude industries like cat-gut spinning. "If stinks and nastiness will infect a town," he comments sarcastically, "it is owing to nothing but the wonders of God's goodness that this place (Southwark side especially) should be at any time free from infection."[23]

These are not new complaints about any city, nor are they uniquely Defoe's in the eighteenth century. Alongside the pamphlets and poems celebrating London's greatness there had grown up after the fire of 1666 an extensive literature of denunciation. Its lineage can be traced back in England at least as far as Thomas Dekker's *Gull's Hornbook* (1609), a witty exposé of London immorality thinly disguised as a moral Baedecker; but its starting point in our period is Ned Ward's raucous serial *The London Spy* (1699), whose popular and financial success bred a host of imitations in the ensuing decades, many of them reprinted year after year, with such beguiling titles as *The Devil upon Crutches in England; or, Night Scenes in London* (1755), *The Vices of the Cities of London and Westminster* (1751), *Hell upon Earth; or, The Town in an Uproar* (1729), *The Tricks of the Town Laid Open; or, A Companion for Country Gentlemen* (1747). The pattern of such guidebooks is always the same: a jerky survey of fleshpots and landmarks—bagnios, playhouses, taverns, and gambling dens—with intermittent, unconvincing censure. Some of them still make wonderful reading—*Hell upon Earth*, for example, thunders in its subtitle against "The late horrible Scenes of Forgery, Perjury, Street-Robbery, Murder, Sodomy, and other shocking Impieties"; and laments that in modern London citizens are "almost under the Necessity of carrying Pistols instead of Prayer-Books to their Parish Churches." And if it all sounds familiar to twentieth-century readers, the book itself has a contemporary, Joycean ring.

This great, wicked, unweildy, over-grown Town, one continued hurry of Vice and Pleasure; where nothing dwells

but *Absurdities, Abuses, Accidents, Accusations, Admirations, Adventures, Adversities, Advertisements, Adulteries, Affidavits, Affectations, Affirmations, Afflictions, Affronts, Aggravations, Agitations, Agonies, Airs, Alarms, Ailments, Allurements, Alterations, Ambitions, Amours, Amphitheatres, Anathemas, Animosities, Anxieties, Appointments, Apprehensions, Arrests, Arrogances, Assassinations, Assemblies, Assessments, Assurances, Assignations, Attainders, Audacities, Aversions,* &c.[24]

We owe much of what we know about the social history of the eighteenth century to these ephemeral pamphlets, but we can also perceive in them, in their numbers and their uniformity, an emerging picture of London as wicked, brutal, and ultimately unmanageable. Even when allowance is made for the period's fascination with low-life—a reaction in part to its Augustan pretensions—the London of these years comes to seem substantially different from the London of Shakespeare or Dekker or Milton. Its size, of course, alters conditions: in 1700 the population is estimated at 674,000, compared with perhaps 200,000 in 1600; and the growth of its boundaries from the City walls east and west was a constant source of astonishment.[25] And too, by the early years of the century an ever more complex capitalism, centered in London's markets and banks, was dealing out its inequities in the city with an increasingly heavy hand. More sober observers, in fact, confirm the general accuracy of the pamphleteers' tirades, and a small anthology of the city's misery could be easily compiled. Henry Fielding, whose work as magistrate in Bow Street brought him as close as Defoe to the life of the streets, reaches an indignant pitch:

Whoever indeed considers the Cities of *London* and *Westminster,* with the late vast Addition of their Suburbs; the great Irregularity of their Buildings, the immense Number of Lanes, Alleys, Courts and Bye-places; must think, that, had they been intended for the very Purpose of Concealment, they could scarce have been better contrived. Upon such a View, the whole appears as a vast Wood or Forest, in which a Thief may harbour with as great Security, as wild Beasts do in the Desarts of *Africa* or *Arabia*.[26]

Ben Sedgly creates a verbal equivalent of Hogarth's "Gin Lane":

> No man can take a survey of this opulent city, without meeting in his way, many melancholy instances resulting from this consumption of spirituous liquors: . . . poverty, diseases, misery, and wickedness, are the daily observations to be made in every part of this great metropolis: whoever passes along the streets, may find numbers of abandoned wretches stretched upon the cold pavement, motionless and insensible, removed only by the charity of passengers from the danger of being crushed by carriages, trampled by horses, or strangled with filth in the common sewers: others may be seen less helpless, perhaps, but more dangerous, who have drank too much to fear punishment, though not enough to hinder them from provoking it. . . .[27]

Less sympathetically, Mandeville snaps at "one of the greatest inconveniences of such vast over-grown Cities as *London* or *Paris*, that they harbour Rogues and Villains as Granaries do Vermin. . . ."[28]

But Mandeville can recite London's disadvantages—"the multitudes of Horses and other Cattle that are always dawbing the Streets, the Carts, Coaches and more heavy Carriages . . . and above all the numberless swarms of People that are continually harrassing and trampling"—and nonetheless accept them as the disadvantages of energy: they result from "the Plenty, great Traffic and Opulency of that mighty City." "Dirty Streets," he insists, "are a necessary Evil inseparable from the Felicity of London."[29] Defoe hangs back from so explicit, so cheerfully amoral a statement, for he finds it difficult, even impossible to reconcile his vision of the city's commercial greatness and his perception of its mundane, poverty-scarred realities. And yet in his fiction if not his journalism, the theme of London's corruption takes on a new form, and he goes past mere approval or disapproval to

fashion its low-life and poverty into an imaginative scene—
the wilderness and forests and oceans of the pamphleteers are
no longer inert metaphors in *Moll Flanders* or *Colonel Jack:*
decisively for English literature, in Defoe's hands the great
city becomes a new setting for stories of voyage and adventure, preeminently for stories of crime.

IV

There exists a special compatibility between the kind of
novels Defoe wrote and the environment that early eighteenth-
century London provided. Narratives of adventure and piracy
like *Robinson Crusoe* (1719), *Captain Singleton* (1720), and
Memoirs of a Cavalier (1720) naturally range widely in their
action, across Africa, the Seven Seas, or England; but increasingly after these works Defoe centers his fiction in his
native city: *Moll Flanders* (1722), *Colonel Jack* (1722), and
Roxana (1724) are all grounded in London, and traditional
episodes of adventure only radiate outward from it, like
spokes in a wheel. The adventurer or pirate becomes, if not
precisely "domesticated," as Paul Zweig suggests, at least
urbanized; and inevitably the time-honored conventions of
such stories are transformed by their urban settings.[30] For
the "wilderness" of London differs sufficiently from an actual
wilderness to thrust new challenges and then new themes
upon a hero; it replaces the exotic beasts, the sirens, and
castles of older adventure with sharpers and slickers, harlots,
and storefronts, and its battles and explorations tend to grow
less and less corporeal and more and more psychological.

One example of such a transformation springs directly from
the facts of London geography. Steen Rasmussen remarks
that great cities are of two physical types, either concen-
trated or scattered, and that London, unlike other European
capitals, is a scattered city.[31] The haphazard development of
urban "squares" during our period—the first was Covent
Garden in 1630—contributed significantly to this sense of
sprawl, and the story of London's growth could be told in
large part by the histories of these projects, whose names lead
us on a knotted trail north and west from the ancient City:

Bedford Square, Soho Square, St. James's Square, Berkeley, Grosvenor, Portman, Cavendish, and many others. Such unplanned, privately controlled growth reflects the democratic, capitalistic nature of eighteenth-century English society, and Rasmussen rightly contrasts it with the principles of absolutism reflected in the systematic design of cities like Paris or Berlin. But this disorderliness also encouraged rapid growth simply for the sake of rapid profits, and particularly the large poor and working-class districts east of St. Paul's and the Royal Exchange continued throughout the century to grow as if at will, with no orderly architectural punctuation at all. The consequences of London's unique shapelessness are quickly felt in the lives of its citizens and its literature. We begin to hear of the unconnectedness of life in the city—not from the great Tory writers like Swift and Pope, to be sure, or from Whig rivals like Addison and Steele, who foster instead a sense of community through the clubs and portraits of the *Spectator* and the *Tatler*. But in the pamphlets of denunciation, the travelogues of low-life, and especially in Defoe's novels we feel emerging those ideas of urban loneliness and anxiety that we now think of as characteristically modern. The images of forests and labyrinths applied to the city suggest not only adventure, but also some of the meanings we currently invoke with words like alienation and anonymity when we describe a megalopolis. Defoe's London has achieved a size and a character that trouble the social life of its people—hence perhaps so many of those attacks on the head grown too great for the body—and more and more frequently we encounter complaints of indifference, of lostness within it.

The crowds that rush continually through the London streets thus become in the eighteenth century a familiar symbol for disintegration of community. More even than the endless streets and low cramped buildings gnarled eastward from the Strand, London's turbulent, unceasing stream of humanity dissolves the fixed relationships of ordinary life and casts individuals adrift. With his sensitivity to the possibilities of loneliness in any situation, Defoe sometimes counterpoints the massiveness of the crowd with a reverie of solitude. "I can affirm," says Robinson Crusoe, "that I enjoy much more solitude in the middle of the greatest collection of man-kind in the world, I mean, at London, while I am writing this, than ever I could say I enjoyed in eight and twenty years' confinement to a desolate island."[32] But Defoe also goes beyond such Puritan acceptance of aloneness to exploit the crowd for other purposes. "It is no accident," writes Paul Zweig, "that the adventurers were drawn to cities like Paris, Venice, Amsterdam, Saint Petersburg, and London, for they embodied an aberrant version of the new urban mentality. Like Robinson Crusoe they were devoted to self-creation, though in the mode of sham. Like Defoe, their identities were pseudonymous, as much to protect as to define themselves. No longer depending on social function or the family or the land for their 'names,' they invented them from the debris of used-out traditions, the way Crusoe invented himself from the debris of his shipwreck."[33] The scale of solitude in so vast a city as London, in other words, raises in a new way questions of personal identity; and though violence and a certain picaresque brutality characterize much of the eighteenth-century literature of lawlessness, a logical theme of Defoe's urban stories is therefore disguise. Moll Flanders enters the wilderness of London in the same way Odysseus enters Phaiakia or Ithaka: "skilled in all ways of contending," expert in false identities. And the size of London, like the size of the sea, absorbs them and makes such adventure possible:

> . . . tho' I often robb'd with these People, yet I never let them know who I was, or where I Lodg'd; nor could they ever find out my Lodging, tho' they often endeavor'd to Watch me to it. They all knew me by the Name of *Moll Flanders,* tho' even some of them rather believ'd I was she, than knew me to be so; my Name was publick among them indeed; but how to find me out they knew not, nor so much as how to guess at my Quarters, whether they were at the East-End of the Town, or the West. [221–22]

She and Roxana and Colonel Jack glide through the crowded streets seen and unseen as they choose, intent only upon survival and willing to invent any part of themselves—their names, their pasts, their appearances—in order to succeed. Like Meneláos, these urban voyagers early meet and master Proteus.

Of course, Defoe's own personality—his habitual caution and self-protectiveness—accounts in part for the exploitation of London anonymity in his novels; but other eighteenth-century writers likewise encounter, even if indirectly, these same issues of urban identity and confusion. *The Beggar's Opera,* for example, can be understood from one point of view as an allegory of city disguise; and the pamphlets on London vice often warn country visitors against believing what they see and hear in the city. "The folly of affectation prevails in London more particularly," we hear in *The Cheats of London Exposed,* "because, through its vast extent, and the multitude of its inhabitants, persons can carry on a disguise with more plausibility, than in towns where the character and circumstances of individuals are minutely inquired into."[34] In the city people meet and deal with each other in impersonal ways, as Defoe well recognizes, according to the model of sales and trade; in the thousand miserable warrens of Wapping or Southwark or in the darkened, unpoliced streets the model is inverted, and one is freer than ever to become and behave as one wishes, to deceive and impose. (In 1736, for example, a new act for the lighting of London streets added about 15,000 lamps, requiring them to be placed at every tenth house from Michaelmas to Lady Day; but certain "light nights" calculated according to the moon were passed each month with no lighting whatsoever.) These variations on the idea of imposture are clearly linked to the presence of theater in the city—a point we will return to in the next chapter—as well as to its opportunities for crime; they represent more or less social responses to the crowds, the disconnections, the freedom of London. But human life is rarely content to persist in disconnections and disunity. "The opaque complexity of modern city life," Raymond

Williams notes, "is represented by crime." In Defoe's novels
and in the low-life pamphlets our experience of London's
social confusion tends to be unified by the drive of characters like Moll or Jack or the country gull to survive in it; the
dimensions of adventure are reduced to theft and prostitution, its terms to property and banknotes; the consciousness
of the Londoner, either victim or offender, is centered upon
crime. (In the nineteenth century and afterward, it is the
figure of the detective and not the Defoean outlaw who unifies the city. "Prefigured in a minor way in Dickens and
Wilkie Collins," Williams says, the detective "now begins to
emerge as a significant and ratifying figure; the man who can
find his way through the fog, who can penetrate the intrica-
cies of the streets.")[35]

One further image of connectedness can be found in Defoe's
London, offsetting all those diffuse anxieties about both the
chaotic wickedness of the city and the uncertainties of the
marketplace.

> *Newgate;* that horrid Place! my very Blood chills at the
> mention of its Name; the Place, where so many of my
> Comrades had been lock'd up, and from whence they went
> to the fatal Tree; the Place where my Mother suffered so
> deeply, where I was brought into the World, and from
> whence I expected no Redemption, but by an infamous
> Death: To conclude, the Place that had so long expected
> me, and which with so much Art and Success I had so
> long avoided. [273]

Moll Flanders's terror at the prospect of Newgate—her "most
forcibly urged emotion," Schorer rather cruelly says—is all
the more compelling in the light of Defoe's other images
of it, for in his fiction and in his biographical pamphlets
about celebrated criminals such as Jonathan Wild and John
Shepperd, he reveals a continuing fascination with incarcera-
tion and escape; Newgate looms ominously in the path of all
his characters, literally as in Moll's case and Jack's and
Roxana's, metaphorically as in Crusoe's island. Defoe shares
the image of confinement with many other eighteenth-century

writers—"I have a prison-scene," runs the prologue to *The Beggar's Opera,* "which the ladies always reckon charmingly pathetic"—and these scenes occupy an understandable prominence in the literature of an age so given to sermonizing. But often enough the image of the prison also contains recognizably urban associations. Moll's first reaction to Newgate echoes an eighteenth-century commonplace: "the hellish Noise, the Roaring, Swearing and Clamour, the Stench and Nastiness, and all the dreadful croud of Afflicting things that I saw there; joyn'd together to make the Place seem an Emblem of Hell itself, and a kind of an Entrance into it" (274). Possibly we may hear echoes of the noises of London too, which are likewise commonly compared to the uproar of hell. But we notice primarily that the ancient convention of an adventurer's visit to the underworld has been invoked. The criminal classes through which Moll moves, or Macheath, constitute a social equivalent of hell already, an extended, fluid underworld. Newgate, however, condenses the ironies of class structure into a symbol for the entire city, and the crowded completeness of the society Moll finds there only bolsters our sense of its infernal urbanity. Another example, Fleet prison, which had its own coffeehouse, apartments, shops, and chapel, is carefully described in Smollett's *Peregrine Pickle* as "like a city detached from all communication with the neighbouring parts, regulated by its own laws, and furnished with peculiar conveniences for the use of the inhabitants." Detachment from neighboring parts and an illusion of self-sufficiency are its essential urban features here, and suggest why some twentieth-century scholars have taken the prison as a model for the city itself: a citadel which at once protects and contains, and a closed system whose inhabitants depend blindly upon a governing authority for food, sanitation, and "conveniences."[36]

In our context, however, entrance into prison occurs as the logical consequence of both commerce and crime, of debt and theft. Other negative images of London, such as the polluted Thames or the giant body, though they irritate the texture of Defoe's portrait, lack the centrality of the prison: it connotes the city in a physical way—its walls parody the city's walls, its population mirrors the desperate population outside, its gates contain, as Moll learns, another London, as inhospitable and as labyrinthine as the one she had departed. Symbolically Newgate stands opposite the Exchange, just as in the landscape of myth the dark prison of a demonic city stands opposite the bright temple of a heavenly one. It is paradoxical to find the experience of the city compressed into such an emblem of enclosure and punishment, when that same experience has also been represented as liberating and creative. Perhaps the coexistence of these contrary meanings in the pages of a single writer—a single book—can be partially explained by reference to the very ancient ambiguity that adventurers have felt toward cities: places (female spaces, Zweig points out) which allure heroic characters toward a life of community, but which end by repelling them toward new adventure, as Odysseus is supposed by Dante to have yielded to wanderlust and to have left Penelope and Ithaka a second time. But the prisons that dot Defoe's London are psychological as well as social; his characters continually barricade themselves, in disguises like Moll Flanders or in fortresses like Robinson Crusoe. We may do better to search for the roots of the city-prison in the alienation that is inseparable from the freedom of the city, the inward solitude that is such a freedom's condition and its consequence. From some unreachable interior landscape Defoe seems almost to project his prisons onto the external screen of the city.

V

Defoe's greatest rendering of London, the dreadful city of prison and death he imagines in *A Journal of the Plague Year*, releases across a full-scale canvas the scattered images of London we have been assembling. The *Journal* belongs to the ancient family of stories that depict a city under siege, of course, a genre that begins with the *Iliad*, and within that family to the special branch in which a city surrenders to an internal enemy rather than to an advancing army. Thucydides' *History*, Lucretius's *De rerum natura*, Boccaccio's *Decameron*—

Defoe's *Journal* stands in this line, but firmly linked to the more general theme of a civilization collapsing upon itself. The theme fascinated the eighteenth century as much as any age—it is foreshadowed in Defoe's own very early account of a natural attack upon London, *The Storm* (1704)—and if the *Journal* does not correspond directly to the *Dunciad* or to Gibbon's *Decline and Fall,* it opens a way toward them.

The most obvious image for the city that Defoe evokes is that of the body. Indeed, plague makes possible the ultimate version of the city as human body grown morbidly unhealthy, a body in which the vital circulation of trade has halted and the great heart of the nation ceased to pump, a victim whose outsized head totters, who kneels and falls forward stricken. The London of his *Journal* becomes for us a living being, not simply a grid of traffic; a gigantic creature suffering, flailing, weeping, dying, which can only be likened to ourselves. Defoe's language raises this human image everywhere—in the names for fever and infection that dot each page, and more explicitly in passages like this one close to the beginning of the book:

> The Face of *London* was now indeed strangely alter'd, I mean the whole Mass of Buildings, City, Liberties, Suburbs, *Westminster, Southwark* and altogether; for as to the particular Part called the City, or within the Walls, that was not yet much infected; but in the whole, the Face of Things, I say, was much alter'd; Sorrow and Sadness sat upon every Face; and tho' some Part were not yet overwhelm'd, yet all look'd deeply concern'd. . . . [16]

The sentence moves from the Face of London to the Face of Things—the buildings—to the Faces of the stricken people; and these are not discriminated among but confusedly identified, so that the inanimate particular and the human ("some Part . . . yet all") fuse in our minds as we read. Defoe calls attention, too, as he often does, to the impossibility of conveying reality through words:

> . . . were it possible to represent those Times exactly to those that did not see them, and give the Reader due

Ideas of the Horror that every where presented it self, it must make just Impressions upon their Minds, and fill them with Surprize. *London* might well be said to be all in Tears; the Mourners did not go about the Streets indeed, for no Body put on black, or made a formal Dress of Mourning for their nearest Friends; but the Voice of Mourning was truly heard in the Streets; the shriecks of Women and Children at the Windows, and Doors of their Houses, where their dearest Relations were, perhaps dying, or just dead, were so frequent to be heard, as we passed the Streets, that it was enough to pierce the stoutest Heart in the World, to hear them. [16]

The language that might achieve such communication is replaced by the shrieks of women and children, by the monotonous, unified Voice of Mourning; the street cries of London and the Babel of its marketplaces will soon give way to the single call, "Bring out your dead," and then to silence. The giant body of London is again personified, for "*London* might well be said to be all in Tears"; but the clause reminds us as well of one great source that Defoe assuredly knew, the descriptions of a ruined Jerusalem in the Old Testament prophecies. "She weepeth sore in the night," Jeremiah cries in Lamentations 10:2, a verse to which Defoe may be alluding, "and her tears are on her cheeks."

Scarcely two pages later, Defoe openly compares Jerusalem besieged at Passover and London struck by plague, both swollen at festive periods, as he says, by an influx of people "who would otherwise have been in other Countries" (18). The same passage sets out for the first time the aspect of the city that will come to trouble him most during the plague year, the mandatory shutting up of houses where sickness was found. A third biblical reference is suggested here, the chapters in Isaiah describing a similar disaster: "The city of confusion is broken down, every house is shut up, that no man may come in. There is a crying for wine in the streets; all joy is darkened, the mirth of the land is gone. In the city is left desolation, and the gate is smitten with destruction" (24:10–12). The situation is the same, but how differently

Defoe proceeds from Isaiah! The prophet's language is generalized. The houses are made to stand for the city, and the city itself is made to suggest the whole nation of Israel. The gate smitten with destruction functions as synecdoche, and we allegorize it into a more general meaning—the city—and even beyond into the terms of the prophet's sermon. But Defoe's sentences are prosaic, freighted with specific names: "The Inns-of-Court were all shut up; nor were very many of the Lawyers in the Temple, or *Lincolns-Inn,* or *Greyes-Inn,* to be seen there. . . . Whole Rows of Houses in some Places, were shut close up; the Inhabitants all fled, and only a Watchman or two left" (17). The artifacts of London are without further significance; the analogy that Defoe recalls between Jerusalem and London is severed abruptly, not linked and complicated as Milton might have forged it. And yet Defoe's unease at the sight of locked houses in the city leads him eventually to expansive metaphor: "here were just so many Prisons in the Town, as there were Houses shut up; and as the People shut up or imprison'd so, were guilty of no Crime, only shut up because miserable, it was really the more intollerable to them" (52).

These prisons come in the course of the *Journal* to symbolize the whole unspeakable disaster of London, for nothing could be more anti-urban than to choke off the traffic and commerce of the city, to prevent its every gesture of community. They are, as Defoe several times points out, prisons without bars and bolts, guarded only by a poor watchman in the street, and their inmates repeatedly escape, leaving dead and dying relatives behind. But London itself has become a gigantic prison, like its own houses; and the efforts to elude the watchmen are paralleled on a larger scale by everyone, sick or well, who flees the city, duping officials along the turnpikes and suspicious villagers in the suburbs. Inside the locked houses family relationships are destroyed by imprisonment, just as outside the normal life of London utterly vanishes: "whole Streets seem'd to be desolated, and not to be shut up only, but to be emptied of their Inhabitants; Doors were left open, Windows stood shattering with the Wind in empty Houses, for want of People to shut them" (171). Grass grows

in the pavement of the Exchange. The shops are closed, the
churches empty. Even those who are not infected retreat behind barricades; H. F. describes an enclosure quite as elaborate and fear-inspired as Crusoe's:

> Dr. *Heath* coming to visit me, and finding that I ventured
> so often out in the Streets, earnestly perswaded me to
> lock my self up and my Family, and not to suffer any of
> us to go out of Doors; to keep all our Windows fast, Shut-
> ters and Curtains close, and never to open them. . . . I went
> and bought two Sacks of Meal, and for several Weeks . . .
> we baked all our own Bread; also I bought Malt, and
> brew'd as much Beer as all the Casks I had would hold,
> and which seem'd enough to serve my House for five or
> six Weeks; also I laid in a Quantity of Salt-butter and
> *Cheshire* Cheese. [77]

And because the city has become a prison, it is all the more
appropriate that the "Crimes" of London are daily lamented
as the cause of God's dreadful punishment.

In such a context, we may think of Moll Flanders's description of Newgate, how it hardens her to misdeed and fear in
the same way that the plague hardens Londoners, and how
prison seems to offer only one certain escape: "I LIV'D
many Days here under the utmost horror of Soul; I had
Death as it were in view, and thought of nothing Night and
Day, but of Gibbets and Halters, evil Spirits and Devils; it is
not to be express'd by Words how I was harrass'd, between
the dreadful Apprehensions of Death, and the Terror of my
Conscience reproaching me with my past horrible Life" (277).
For Moll, Crusoe, Colonel Jack, all of infected London, prison
leads toward its own symbol: the "terrible Pit" dug in the
churchyard of Aldgate to receive the dead of the parish.
H. F. cannot resist his curiosity to see this "dreadful Gulph"
(59), which threatens to swallow the city:

> . . . some blam'd the Church-Wardens for suffering such a
> frightful Thing, telling them they were making Prepara-
> tions to bury the whole Parish, and the like; but Time
> made it appear, the Church-Wardens knew the Condition

of the Parish better than they did; for the Pit being finished the 4th of *September,* I think, they began to bury in it the 6th, and by the 20th, which was just two Weeks they had thrown into it 1114 Bodies. [59]

The image of the crowd makes a final, macabre, uncommunicative appearance as he goes to see where 400 new victims have been buried and to watch the dead cart empty its load:

the Cart had in it sixteen or seventeen Bodies, some were wrapt up in Linen Sheets, some in Rugs, some little other than naked, or so loose, that what Covering they had, fell from them, in the shooting out of the Cart, and they fell quite naked among the rest; but the Matter was not much to them, or the Indecency much to any one else, seeing they were all dead, and were to be huddled together into the common Grave of Mankind. . . . [62]

This pit and a dozen others in scattered districts—like the underworlds of epic—complete London's transformation into a demonic city, just as they complete the symbolism of prison. A massive, common grave is what London has become, as H. F. sits in the window of his own locked house and scans the still streets below, a metaphor to summarize the city under judgment.

VI

The vision of London set down in the *Journal,* a vision bodied forth in its remorseless images of sickness, prison, and grave, haunts every modern reader: no later artist of catastrophe has surpassed Defoe's creative truthfulness here; it may even be doubted whether those other fables of disaster and rescue, *Robinson Crusoe* and *Moll Flanders,* touch our apprehensions quite so nearly. But as we turn over in our minds the effects of the *Journal*—the anecdotes of terror and loneliness, the vignettes of a collapsing city—it becomes possible to think of Defoe's vision in another way: is this not only London as it is in plague, but also London as it always is?

Bubonic plague spreads imperceptibly, through the infection of fleas by rats and men by fleas; men rarely infect each other. To seventeenth-century London, however, the disease seemed to pass mysteriously from person to person in the ordinary course of daily life. "The Opinion of the Physicians agreed with my Observation afterwards," H. F. says, "namely, that the Danger was spreading insensibly; for the Sick cou'd infect none but those that came within reach of the sick Person; but that one Man, who may have really receiv'd the Infection, and knows it not, but goes Abroad, and about as a sound Person, may give the Plague to a thousand People" (195). And again: "These were the dangerous People, these were the People of whom the well People ought to have been afraid; but then *on the other side* it was impossible to know them" (191). Other contemporary historians of the plague record this same phenomenon, but alone among them Defoe relentlessly transforms it into a metaphor for social alienation:

> I knew a Man who conversed freely in *London* all the Season of the Plague in 1665, and kept about him an Antidote or Cordial, on purpose to take when he thought himself in any Danger, and he had such a Rule to know . . . as indeed I never met with before or since. . . . He had a Wound in his Leg, and whenever he came among any People that were not sound, and the Infection began to affect him, he said he could know it by that Signal, (*viz.*) That his Wound in his Leg would smart. . . . Now it seems he found his Wound would smart many Times when he was in Company with such, who thought themselves to be sound, and who appear'd so to one another; but he would presently rise up, and say publickly, Friends, here is some Body in the Room that has the Plague, and so would immediately break up the Company. [191–92]

Such breaking up of company, numberless other acts of suspicion and fear, the hostility of walkers in the streets—all these arise naturally from the ravages of plague, but it requires only the slightest shift in focus to see these states of mind present in the normal city as well. "Dread and anxiety are the central emotions examined" in the *Journal,* observes Austin Flanders; and these might be typical urban emotions at any time; "a universal fear of human contact is the creeping moral and psychological malady which Defoe chronicles."[37] It is a fear well documented by urban sociologists: like Defoe's barricaded houses, the chain-locked apartments of New York or Chicago testify to community in distress, community at the edge of breakdown. The bands of marauding robbers and bullying youths that H. F. remembers in London's streets can be duplicated in any great modern city—the Mohocks reveal exactly this strain in ordinary eighteenth-century life—as can the poor and defeated who die untended in corners and alleys. It may be objected that to see Defoe's book in this way is to allegorize it where no allegory was intended, to confuse Defoe's manner with Camus's or Thucydides', who permit a range of interpretation foreign to his style. But much in the *Journal* seems to confirm these liberties, and to stretch back toward Defoe's other representations of London.

The attention he gives to the breakdown of London's economy, for example, recalls his anxiety for the stability of prosperity at any time. Thus Flanders compares the paralysis of London trade to an economic depression, the bust that follows boom, and suggests that Defoe is unconsciously describing the workings of urban capitalism. His account of this aspect of the plague is especially detailed and sympathetic, after all: he lists carefully the classes of tradesmen thrown into distress by the disappearance of customers and itemizes the small manufactures and merchandising that suffered. When the building or repairing of houses stopped, to extract from one such table, it thereby turned *"all the ordinary Work-men of that Kind out of Business; such as Brick-layers, Masons, Carpenters, Joyners, Plasterers, Painters, Glaziers, Smiths, Plumbers; and all the Labourers depending on such"* (95). And where trade did not actually halt—as in the sale of food—*"All Families retrench'd their living as much as possible,"* releasing superfluous servants and journeymen (95). Defoe pays tribute to the outpouring of charity that sustained so many of the unemployed, but he also reports that when they received no help or not enough, like Moll herself,

the poor began to steal; and he sketches brief, frightening
scenes of mobs, hungry and crazed, looting the warehouses
and abandoned homes of the prosperous. The transformation
of the unemployed into criminals (or ironically into watchmen for the city's "prisons") reminds us of this same transformation in Defoe's fiction. Business itself, the "great Trade
in the City" (19), has drawn so many outlanders into London;
and business now ruins them. Even where commerce does
continue, plague serves to bring out those fears Defoe seems
always alert to: the potential for estrangement implicit in
the mechanical, impersonal relationships of ordinary trade,
for instance, is intensified—

> when any one bought a Joint of Meat in the Market, they
> would not take it of the Butchers Hand, but take it off
> of the Hooks themselves. On the other Hand, the Butcher
> would not touch the Money, but have it put into a Pot
> full of Vinegar which he kept for that purpose. [78]

"This Necessity of going out of our Houses to buy Provisions,"
H. F. claims, "was in a great Measure the Ruin of the whole
City" (78). If it is too ingenious to link the appearance of
disease in the market with the hypocrisy of normal trade, we
can still recognize this same sense of uncertainty, of dangerous false pretenses and false dealing, disclosed in other discussions like *The Complete English Tradesman* of how to
survive in business.

Persuasive as is the case for seeing H. F.'s London as an
emblem of urban capitalism, it nonetheless seems incomplete. The impact of the *Journal* is too visceral, too immediate to be fully explained by economic fears alone; it
touches too many other human concerns. The shutting up
of the houses evokes associations of the tomb as well as of
debtor's prison; the unraveling of family ties and all ordinary
social relationships wrenches those who remain in the city
into an unimaginable, uncommercial loneliness. In particular,
the mesmerism of London's poor during this time by quack
astrologers, widely documented in chronicles of the plague,
can be taken as one further instance of civic disintegration,

of retreat from urban pressures and realities into a collective madness. But from another perspective, the rekindling of superstition, which H. F. snappishly condemns, is typical of every city at every time. For the city, as Jacques Ellul reminds us, is in the Bible a cursed place.[38] Built first by Cain in defiance of God's order, its original intention was to exclude God from its boundaries; and in the Old Testament, Babylon, Jerusalem, and all secular cities are archetypal seats of corruption, endlessly subject to catastrophe. They are also always repositories of superstition, because superstition and magic represent attempts, like Cain's, to master (or imitate) divine powers; the idolatry of Babylon in Isaiah 47 typically replaces the worship of the true God with the worship of man-made gods. And if this point of view finds few endorsements in the twentieth century, it is all the more important to recall how natural it seemed to a society like early eighteenth-century England, and especially to a writer of the Puritan tradition like Defoe. The allegory a modern reader may search for in the plague might be political or economic or sociological; the interpretation Defoe points toward is religious: God sent the plague to punish a wicked city. Sickness only makes visible on the external body the inner moral disease of London; the plague rages like a fever or a great fire, deliberately, furiously, as if to castigate: "if a few Houses only are contiguous where it happens," it "can only burn a few Houses. . . . But if it begins in a close built Town, or City, and gets a Head, there its Fury encreases, it rages over the whole Place, and consumes all it can reach" (198). In the angry, unforgiving plague is the fullest possible expression of the theme of London corruption. H. F. scorns the old women who follow magicians promising protection or cure through London streets; but he accepts the plague as God's manifest judgment—he can even wish it sterner and longer lasting.

Just as in the *Tour,* however, when he so carefully describes the real glory of London and the Thames, Defoe would not be misunderstood as fanciful or irrational. In the early days of the plague, H. F., who generally speaks with his author's voice, joins a crowd in the street, all staring up into the Air, to see what a Woman told them appeared plain to her, which was an Angel cloth'd in white, with a fiery Sword in his Hand, waving it, or brandishing it over his Head. She described every Part of the Figure to the Life; shew'd them the Motion, and the Form; and the poor People came into it so eagerly, and with so much Readiness; YES, *I see it all plainly,* says one. *There's the Sword as plain as can be.* Another saw the Angel. One saw his very Face, and cry'd out, What a glorious Creature he was! One saw one thing, and one another. I look'd as earnestly as the rest, but, perhaps, not with so much Willingness to be impos'd upon; and I said indeed, that *I could see nothing,* but a white Cloud, bright on one Side, by the shining of the Sun upon the other Part. [22–23]

(It is an incident of insistent factualness that we may wish to contrast with a visionary moment in Blake: "What it will be Questiond When the Sun rises do you not see a round Disk of fire somewhat like a Guinea O no no I see an Innumerable company of the Heavenly host crying Holy Holy Holy is the Lord God Almighty.")[39] And yet despite H. F.'s literalness, the care he takes in distinguishing among various theories of infection, the statistics, the convincing detail—despite all these, the impression a reader may at last take away from the *Journal* is less one of verisimilitude than of unreality. Defoe's imaginative works tend always to subvert the pious, orderly declarations of his moral writings and journalism; his presentation of plague-stunned London is clogged with numbers and facts, but the effect of it all is not so much of a man thinking as of a man dreaming; his calculations numb, and in the process release a vision truly more frightening and less coherent than Blake's, a nightmare.

As we ponder the dreamlike atmosphere of the *Journal,* the effect that comes finally to dominate is our feeling of lost control; the plague comes or goes as mysteriously as the wind that carries it; the city caves in by piecemeal, like a rotting forest, according to no pattern, beyond all management. Defoe's narration even mirrors this shapelessness, moving restlessly back and forth over his themes as unpredictably as the plague moves over the city. The only possible response, H. F. concludes, is to surrender the doomed and unpredictable city and seek the country: *"The best Physick against the Plague is to run away from it"* (197–98). We may think of Juvenal's Umbricius, who also regards the city this way and preaches a pastoral retreat from the falling houses of Rome. But Defoe does not usually frame his pages with classical parallels; his sense of chaotic, warring forces, so heightened by the presence of plague, has a personal dimension instead, and extends to all his other images of London. The city has *always* seemed to him beyond control, in its growth, its lack of form, its economic vagaries; his London, like Pope's, is an external, absolute phenomenon, not molded any longer in human patterns to satisfy human needs, but existing independently, a machine to be stoked, a giant to be pacified. If we consider this loss of control from the coordinates of myth, we may say that in Defoe's vision the very purpose of the city has been overturned: what was formed, as Mircea Eliade says, to exclude chaos has now come to evince it; what the walls of the city once distinguished from the sterility of desert or the darkness of forest now exists as man-made forest and desert, as labyrinth.[40] And if we pursue seriously the analogy between the *Journal* and a dream, we may be willing to see the plague as what, in one mood, Defoe actually wished for the city:

> *Son.* Why, madam, you would put us all into confusion. You would fright and terrify us so that we must shut up our shops, embargo our ships, close our ports; the Custom House would have no business, the Exchange no merchants, the merchandise no market.
> *Mother.* I say again, oh that I could see such a sight in London! It is true it would be as you described it, and indeed it ought to be.[41]

The mother is hoping for a day of national humiliation, but her language nevertheless calls forth a picture of all life in London brought to a halt, the city dead as it deserves to be.

The vehemence of such moments in Defoe seems to result from that impossible insistence we began with in the *Tour* that what he write be literally true. Wordsworth, no friend to London, gives in "The Reverie of Poor Susan" another kind of response to the city, an imagined life instead of death.

> At the corner of Wood Street, when daylight appears,
> Hangs a Thrush that sings loud, it has sung for three years:
> Poor Susan has passed by the spot, and has heard
> In the silence of morning the song of the Bird.
>
> 'Tis a note of enchantment; what ails her? She sees
> A mountain ascending, a vision of trees;
> Bright volumes of vapour through Lothbury glide,
> And a river flows on through the vale of Cheapside.
>
> Green pastures she views in the midst of the dale,
> Down which she so often has tripped with her pail;
> And a single small cottage, a nest like a dove's,
> The one only dwelling on earth that she loves.
>
> She looks, and her heart is in heaven: but they fade,
> The mist and the river, the hill and the shade:
> The stream will not flow, and the hill will not rise,
> And the colours have all passed away from her eyes![42]

Poor Susan is trapped in the city, just as the thrush is imprisoned in its cage and just as H. F. and Moll Flanders are imprisoned. But the thrush sings, and Susan's power of fantasy defeats, for a time at least, the realities of London. She is "poor" in one sense, far from the mountains and streams she imagines; but rich in another, for the city yields to her human pressure before she at last yields to it. Defoe, if the distinction can be allowed, is a writer who projects a vision, while Wordsworth possesses one: Defoe spins his London out of his own anxieties as naturally as a spider spins a web. Pope, to whose London we turn next, likewise looks upon the city as beyond his control and dying, captured by Dunces as completely as by plague. Yet he too possesses a vision. He removes himself to the country like poor Susan or like Wordsworth and at the same time holds fast to that humanistic ideal he speaks of in his letters as an "abiding city."[43] Defoe's London also abides, but in the face of his anger and indifferent to it.

2

Pope's London:
Dultown and Augusta

Like Defoe, Pope sometimes approaches London from the river. *Windsor-Forest* begins far from the great city, both in place and time, invoking the "groves of Eden, vanish'd now so long," and offering to compare them to the green and reassuring order of the forest's beauty.[1]

> Here hills and vales, the woodland and the plain,
> Here earth and water seem to strive again,
> Not Chaos-like together crush'd and bruis'd,
> But, as the world, harmoniously confus'd.
>
> [11–14]

The passage not only introduces the ancient topos of *discors concordia* in the landscape, but also asserts, with an assurance Pope was never quite to match again, the corresponding presence of such order in the social landscape of England; the world of pure pastoral is behind the poet; he now insists, as he will all his life, that the beauty he is gifted to discover bear a relationship to the society he lives in. Windsor Forest symbolizes the political order of England as well as the principle of inclusive order in nature:

> Here Ceres' gifts in waving prospect stand,
> And nodding tempt the joyful reaper's hand;
> Rich Industry sits smiling on the plains,
> And peace and plenty tell, a STUART reigns.
>
> [39–42]

In one of the happiest sentences ever written about Pope, Maynard Mack observes that "Pope's poetry, like the book he was accustomed to call Scripture, begins with a garden and ends with a city."[2] Although Professor Mack refers to the whole sweep of Pope's achievement, from *Pastorals* to final *Dunciad,* the pattern is already formed in miniature in *Windsor-Forest,* where the garden of Eden vanishes a second time toward the end of the poem, to be replaced by the city he and his contemporaries styled "Augusta." The change, occurring in a portion Pope wrote some nine years after the beginning, is carried out by means of another ancient poetic device, a catalogue of rivers:

> In that blest moment from his oozy bed
> Old father Thames advanc'd his rev'rend head.
> His tresses drop'd with dews, and o'er the stream
> His shining horns diffus'd a golden gleam:
> Grav'd on his urn appear'd the moon, that guides
> His swelling waters, and alternate tides;
> The figur'd streams in waves of silver roll'd,
> And on their banks Augusta rose in gold.
>
> [329–36]

The Thames can be understood in a number of ways as an emblem of London—we have seen a few of them briefly in Defoe—and we shall touch on its uses again in this chapter. Here, however, Pope's description of the river helps to fix Augusta in a framework of idealized order. What was lost as garden is promised as city. Father Thames appears in the poem just after "great ANNA," imitating the divine *fiat,* has spoken: " 'Let Discord cease!'/She said, the world obey'd, and all was peace!" (327–28). These daring lines allude, necessarily, to much more than the Peace of Utrecht in 1713. The first third of *Windsor-Forest* has traced the largely dismal, disorderly history of England from the Norman Conquest to the reign of William III, a grim chronicle of destruction and tyranny punctuated with images of "Cities laid waste," "levell'd towns," "broken columns," and "heaps of ruin." The harmonious landscape of the first verses has given way

entirely to the desolated landscape, political and natural, of
an earlier England, one which Pope is careful to compare to
Troy. Even recent history has continued this chaos, with its
civil wars and plague and fire in London: "She saw her sons
with purple deaths expire,/Her sacred domes involv'd in
rolling fire" (323–24). Anna's pronouncement, so welcome
after this lawless past, is as much prophecy as command. The
Thames and its obedient tributaries form a procession eastward from Windsor Forest toward royal London:

> Behold! th' ascending Villa's on my side,
> Project long shadows o'er the crystal tide.
> Behold! Augusta's glitt'ring spires increase,
> And Temples rise, the beauteous works of Peace.
> I see, I see where two fair cities bend
> Their ample bow, a new Whitehall ascend!
> There mighty Nations shall enquire their doom,
> The World's great Oracle in times to come;
> There Kings shall sue, and suppliant States be seen
> Once more to bend before a BRITISH QUEEN.
> [375–84]

The vision of London set down here inevitably reminds us of
others—of the conclusion to Dryden's *Annus Mirabilis,* for
example, which also celebrates an Augusta-Troy rich, majestic, and served by great rivers. (Unlike Defoe, who sees London's markets from Hampton Court, Pope chooses London's
glittering spires and temples and Inigo Jones's Whitehall for
his synecdoche; and for him its shape is bowlike, not monstrous.) But the most immediate source is surely Pope's own
impassioned account, one year earlier in *The Messiah,* of the
New Jerusalem ascending to redeem an anarchic world:

> Rise, crown'd with light, imperial Salem, rise!
> Exalt thy tow'ry head, and lift thy eyes!
> See, a long race thy spacious courts adorn;
> See future sons and daughters yet unborn . . .
> See barb'rous nations at thy gates attend,
> Walk in thy light, and in thy temple bend.
> [85–92]

The conclusion of *Windsor-Forest* like that of *The Messiah* is indebted to Isaiah, as the Thames flows out of London and enters "unbounded" into the sea, stretching the peaceful English empire to every end of the earth.[3] "Unbounded," as Pope himself tells us in a note, refers to his wish that London be made a free port, but it also conveys the sense of expansive order that his vision creates. The river will unify the "confus'd" harmony of the world, will bring political and commercial order to the nations, unite the Old and New Worlds, subordinate wisely ("bend") the savage races now chained in slavery, and restore the golden cathedral of Mexico, a distant and inferior counterpart to steepled London. (Modern readers may recall another such moment, in Conrad's haunting description at the opening of *Heart of Darkness,* where the Thames runs from London outward, "an interminable waterway" that begins at "the biggest, and the greatest, town on earth.") The sixth book of the *Aeneid* lies behind Pope's new prophecy of empire, of course, and together with the others this large allusion gives further well-ordered shape to Anne's London, placing it securely in both literary and political lines of succession. Finally, Pope closes this complex picture of order, whose center is London, with a reiterated image of disorder tamed: "Exil'd . . . to deepest hell" are all those elements of chaos that Eden or Augusta excludes.

> In brazen bonds shall barb'rous Discord dwell;
> Gigantic Pride, pale Terror, gloomy Care,
> And mad Ambition shall attend her there:
> There purple Vengeance bath'd in gore retires,
> Her weapons blunted, and extinct her fires. . . .
>
> [414–18]

But few students of his poetry will fail to recall how such disorderly exile reappears in the banishment and enchaining of Wit, Science, the Muses, and Morality beneath Dulness's footstool in the fourth book of the *Dunciad.*

I

The London so briefly but beautifully imaged in *Windsor-Forest* is obviously an ideal city, not a "real" one such as we might tour in Stow's *Survey* or John Rocque's maps, or even in Defoe's *Journal:* one of several names—Rome, as "Augusta" reminds us, is another—for that abiding city on which Pope very early set his gaze. This London belongs to a profoundly ancient tradition, a conception of civilized community that finds expression at every level of literature, from Virgil to the hymnist's "Who Shall Paint That Lovely City?" Here Evelyn Waugh invokes it in his novel *Helena,* describing the wall that divides Gaul from barbaric Germany:

> Think of it, mile upon mile, from snow to desert, a single great girdle round the civilized world; inside, peace, decency, the law, the altars of the Gods, industry, the arts, order; outside, wild-beasts and savages, forest and swamp, bloody mumbo-jumbo, men like wolf-packs; and along the wall the armed might of the Empire, sleepless, holding the line. Doesn't it make you see what The City means?[4]

All order includes the compulsion to repeat. Mircea Eliade suggests that the first cities built on earth had as their deepest purpose, their mythic meaning, something like Waugh's vision, the exclusion of chaos and the reproduction of the heavenly city of the gods, where order was enthroned and a life free from destruction and disintegration was possible.[5] Pope's Augusta, whatever its ultimate origins, embodies a similar idea of order. The description in *Windsor-Forest* places the city in the widest imaginable context, at the center of a harmonizing, civilizing force that is literally global, one that repeats the civilizing work of earlier cities like Rome and at the same time (as the presence of pagan gods and the allusions to Isaiah make plain) imitates the divine civilization.

Explanation for the intense appeal of this vision of order to Pope may have to be grounded finally in personality, but we can easily name the chief literary sources that strengthened the habit: the seventeenth-century English poets who pondered England's destiny through a long period of civil war; the noble cities of order in Isaiah and Revelation; above all, the vision of eternal Rome that he absorbed from the Latin classics and that, considerably coarsened, was routinely invoked

everywhere in early eighteenth-century England as an analogy
with London. It would be a mistake, I think, to underestimate
the importance of this ideal city of order for Pope. To trace
it dispassionately back along the tracks of religious anthro-
pology or literary history, to state abstractly its intellectual
content, to label it simply "order"—all this may distract us
from seeing how vividly real it is for him. Pope's celebration
of "ORDER" has been one cause for modern resistance to
his poetry, as any teacher of eighteenth-century literature can
confirm; he encounters head-on a widespread distaste for the
regulation and repression implied by the word and by the
couplet form that appears to mirror it. But Pope's city of
order, though it must overcome resistant parts, also depends
upon a principle of interrelatedness:

> So from the first eternal ORDER ran,
> And creature link'd to creature, man to man.
> Whate'er of life all-quick'ning aether keeps,
> Or breathes thro' air, or shoots beneath the deeps,
> Or pours profuse on earth; one nature feeds
> The vital flame, and swells the genial seeds.
>   [*An Essay on Man*, III, 113–18]

If we do no more than gloss lines like these by references to
the Great Chain of Being, we risk overlooking how urgently
Pope works to incorporate as well as to repress and repeat:
the elements of any scene, whether of Windsor Forest or the
whole bounds of Being, must be fitted into a Whole, a One
that permits both relationships and completeness. Hence the
garden and the city are often equivalent symbols for him,
both of them human organizations that stand in opposition
to the wilderness outside their walls. This consciousness of
the Whole, of man's indefatigably social nature, is characteristic of the age in general, as every student quickly recognizes;
but it is especially characteristic of Pope. No one who reads
his letters can fail to think of him this way, I imagine, constantly calling together, reaching out toward his myriad cor-
respondents, continually building community; the virtue of
friendship so often the subject of these letters arouses him

powerfully, perhaps among other reasons because it is a means toward seeing his and other lives whole. Pope's Augusta is a secular city quite as much as a divine imitation, one where every detail, even the tax status of the port of London, must be incorporated into the whole, in part to exclude chaos, but also in part to call forth a living order.

And yet the call for regulation is there, too, indispensably. We hear it in another metaphor for the city, a favorite in the eighteenth century and after its fashion as classical as Augustine's or Virgil's. Lewis Thomas gives a twentieth-century version of that timeless image of human collectivity, the anthill:

> What makes us most uncomfortable is that they, and the bees and termites and social wasps, seem to live two kinds of lives: they are individuals, going about the day's business without much evidence of thought for tomorrow, and they are at the same time component parts, cellular elements, in the huge, writhing, ruminating organism of the Hill, the nest, the hive.[6]

It is an obviously less grandiose version of Pope's abiding city, alive and orderly. Implicit in Thomas's image, however, and never absent from Pope's, is the gravely serious cause of our discomfort at the comparison: the tension between the two kinds of lives, the constant threat that one kind of life—the individual or the collective—will destroy the other. Not merely a collective unity, the form of Pope's city holds in check the elements it contains. The *Essay on Man* names the beehive and the anthill as contrary models for human cities— one monarchical, the other democratic—but stress also falls upon the potentially dangerous selfishness of bees, whose enlightened "Self-love and Reason" providentially

> ... to one end aspire,
> Pain their aversion, Pleasure their desire;
> But greedy That, its object would devour,
> This taste the honey, and not wound the flow'r.
>   [II, 87–90]

From them we are to learn how to reconcile our separate
drives into laws fixed and wise:

> Here too all forms of social union find,
> And hence let Reason, late, instruct Mankind:
> Here subterranean works and cities see;
> There towns aerial on the waving tree.
> Learn each small People's genius, policies,
> The Ant's republic, and the realm of Bees;
> How those in common all their wealth bestow,
> And Anarchy without confusion know;
> And these for ever, tho' a Monarch reign,
> Their sep'rate cells and properties maintain.
> Laws wise as Nature, and as fix'd as Fate.
> [III, 179–90]

Similarly, the best-known eighteenth-century example of the
beehive image, Mandeville's, uses the polarity of virtue and
vice to describe London life; and Pope and Defoe and Gay in
very different ways place underworld and respectable world
in conflict, imposing form upon the city (battlefield, body,
prison) and with form, inevitably, tension.[7]

The tension present whenever heterogeneous parts are
bound into a form has a moral as well as aesthetic dimension,
of course. Maynard Mack speaks of the "existing city" that
stands in opposition to the abiding one, the London of
Walpole and Lintot and Lord Fanny, what Pope increasingly
called simply "the town."[8] In the town, the London most of
us would acknowledge as actual, the hierarchical, regular,
beautiful virtues of Augusta are sapped by the material realities of disease, overcrowding, noise, filth: all the mundane
horrors of urban life, to which Pope more than most men was
sensitive. They alone might be enough to account for the
tarnishing of Augusta in his poetry over the years, except
that, in the satires of the thirties and decisively in the *Dunciad,*
Augusta was not merely dismantled as an ideal; it was transformed, transmogrified into what he once called (perhaps no
less mythically) "That Scene of Folly Militant."[9] His phrase
insures that his reader will understand the importance of

moral decay in the fate of London; for to Pope and his contemporaries the ruin of England as they saw it was centered and symbolized in the sinking capital of London, an existing city whose physical limitations had only come to stand for deeper, irreversibly corrosive limitations of the spirit.

II

It may be that the tendency to imagine an ideal necessarily leads to satire. The poem, we are reminded, with which *Windsor-Forest* falls most naturally into contrast is the *Dunciad.* Urban, satiric, guided by a malevolent goddess, the *Dunciad* too unfolds a prophecy of empire like *Windsor-Forest;* but every step of its prophecy overturns the fabulous, yearning idealism of the earlier poem and replaces it with a nightmarish contraction of the moral life, set down in the streets and halls of a London uniquely Pope's own.

In the pages that follow I want to suggest how three major facets of the Dunces' London—the river, the theater, and language—may be used to establish points of connection, not only with Pope's earlier vision of the city, but also with Defoe, Wordsworth, and Blake. Before turning to these images, however, we may note that no less than Defoe, Pope makes of London an abstract civic space. Aubrey L. Williams's ground-breaking study of the *Dunciad* has called attention to the care with which Pope charted the movement of the Dunces in book II, showing how closely their progress through the city follows the route of the annual Lord Mayor's Day parade; and he has also stressed the satiric purposes behind Pope's imitation of the action of the *Aeneid* in the whole poem, which suggests the invasion and conquest of a city by the forces of Dulness, the establishment of a new unholy *urbs* in Troy-novant.[10] The city thus stormed, of course, is the aristocratic court world that lay along the western curve of the Thames, the part of London symbolized in *Windsor-Forest* by Whitehall and Queen Anne. The City itself, represented in *Windsor-Forest* only by the fifty churches Anne decreed to be built, contains the trading and residential areas within the old walls (still standing then) and the adjoining liberties—the

London, that is, of Defoe and Ned Ward rather than Great Anna. These two sectors were in the early eighteenth century physically distinct: north and west of Charing Cross rapidly developing squares like St. James's, Soho, Golden, Hanover, and Cavendish gave haven for the aristocracy and the most prosperous of the middle classes; east of Temple Bar the crowded, winding alleys and courtyards around St. Paul's, Cheapside, the Tower, Wapping, Hockley Hole enclosed the immemorial haunts of London's poor and, more and more in the eighteenth century, the site of its manufacturers as well as its commerce.[11] These separate cities were chiefly joined—the "ample bow" that Pope and other writers saw— by the Strand, by Oxford Street, and by the river, whose watermen served throughout the century as rapid transport from one end to the other. Every city encloses extremes of poverty and wealth, but the cleavage between West End and City was especially visible and felt in Pope's time, as to some extent it still is today; and the differences between the large-scale, open settings of the one, with its elegant red brick and Portland stone houses of the "first rate" (a taxpayer's term) and handsome squares, and the teeming, close-set houses and shops of the other easily lent themselves to moralizing distinctions. Addison, in fact, compares the different sections of London to different nations in the *Spectator* (403), as do Tom Brown in his *Amusements Serious and Comical* and Sir Richard Steele in *The Tender Husband*. In several senses, then, this division could be taken conveniently to represent a schematic outline for conflict between heavenly and secular cities; the action of the *Dunciad* overthrows the Court of Augusta and establishes in its ruins what Emrys Jones has aptly named "Dultown."[12] The pattern is traditional. Babylon once again takes Jerusalem into its long captivity, but the details are entirely Augustan.

The river that joins the two cities is in Pope's hands an instrument of cruelest parody. The London of *Windsor-Forest,* as we have seen, is continuous with the landscape; its glittering towers rise from the scene like Father Thames and like the trees of the forest itself, forming a complex pattern of imitation and resemblance. In the *Dunciad,* however, city and landscape are neither consecutive, as in *Windsor-Forest,* nor contrasted, as for example in the "Epistle to Miss Blount . . . after the Coronation," but simply unrelated: the *Dunciad* is all urbanity, all people and buildings, the garden and the city are unyoked.

Only the Thames remains to remind us of the disjunction. Professor Jones has rightly pointed out the remarkable geniality of spirit that seems to predominate in the heroic games of book II, the feeling we have that here at least the Dunces behave more like rollicking children than villains, innocently uninhibited and "completely without self-consciousness"; and surely as he says, the vitality of this life, for all its contrast with the adult world Pope normally inhabits, exerts a strong, agreeable pull on his imagination.[13] One aspect of these games, even while it demonstrates exactly this kind of liberation, also recalls to us the rivers that flow eastward from Windsor Forest, and by extension all those rivers of myth and literature that always enter a great city. Pope introduces the river with the memorable word "disemboguing"—

> This labour past, by Bridewell all descend,
> (As morning pray'r, and flagellation end)
> To where Fleet-ditch with disemboguing streams
> Rolls the large tribute of dead dogs to Thames—
>
> [*Dunciad,* II, 269–72]

which he had used on two earlier occasions. We hear "the deep roar of disemboguing *Nile*" in his translation of the *Odyssey* (IV, 480), part of the Proteus episode, which has unsettling connections with the theme of falling cities; and it also occurs in the *Iliad* (XVII, 311), when the doomed Trojans rush toward the Achaians:

> Fierce to the Charge great *Hector* led the Throng;
> Whole *Troy* embodied, rush'd with Shouts along.
> Thus, when a Mountain-Billow foams and raves,
> Where some swoln River disembogues his Waves,
> Full in the Mouth is stopp'd the rushing Tide,
> The boiling Ocean works from Side to Side,

The River trembles to his utmost Shore,
And distant Rocks rebellow to the Roar.[14]

These are heroic associations. In reality the Fleet Ditch was
a river running from Holborn to the Thames, forty feet wide
in places and five feet deep at low tide, a "nauceious and
abominable sink of nastiness," one contemporary bluntly re-
ported, a navigable sewer.[15] It drained some of the most
wretched areas of the City, slums like Grub Street, Moorfields
(the site of Bedlam Hospital), and Snow Hill, all the way
down to Fleet prison; its "black shores," as Gay called them
in *Trivia,* were lined with coal wharves, butcher stalls, and
other small shops, which all contributed to its redoubtable
pollution. Barges and lighters regularly plied as far north as
Holborn Bridge. In the Fleet Ditch's special character we may
catch a further glimpse of that underground motif so prevalent in portraits of the modern city, an ideal introduced
figuratively by the urban "underworld," as in Defoe's adventures, and also by imagery of subways, subterranean rivers,
and gutters. But Pope's interest is chiefly in another direction. This tributary of the Thames reverses altogether the
graceful picture of tributaries in *Windsor-Forest* and of the
"obedient Rivers" at the end of the *Epistle to Burlington.*
In this London the "waves of silver" of Windsor Forest
undergo an antibaptismal greeting from

> The King of dykes! than whom no sluice of mud
> With deeper sable blots the silver flood.
>
> [*Dunciad,* II, 273–75]

The unsavory reputation of Fleet Ditch mocks not only the
strong, wide rivers of the classical world but also those specifically English presentations of London and its river, including Pope's own, that celebrate order rather than mud,
beauty rather than sable streams. Spenser, for example, in the
magnificent pageant of rivers in *The Faerie Queene* (book IV,
canto xi) shows us the Thames wearing triumphantly the dia-
dem of Troy-novant, London's legendary predecessor. And
again in book III, canto ix, London masters the dragonlike
Thames and stands above it in queenly majesty:

It *Troynouant* is hight, that with the waues
Of wealthy *Thamis* washed is along,
Vpon whose stubborne neck, whereat he raues
With roring rage, and sore him selfe does throng,
That all men feare to tempt his billowes strong,
She fastned hath her foot, which standes so hy,
That it a wonder of the world is song
In forreine landes, and all which passen by,
Beholding it from far, doe thinke it threates the skye.[16]

Spenser's verse takes a prominent place in the heroic back-drop against which we see the Dunces' river games, but it is also important to notice how it states the relationship of city and river in symbolically sexual terms, a tradition Pope too draws upon for his satiric purposes. Smedley, who earlier had vanished, now surfaces in a marvelous passage, a dizzying condensation in which we hear echoes of *Aeneid* I and VI, of *Paradise Lost,* even perhaps of Father Thames in *Windsor-Forest,* who rises to turn his gaze upon Augusta:

> . . . Lo! a burst of thunder shook the flood.
> Slow rose a form, in majesty of Mud;
> Shaking the horrors of his sable brows,
> And each ferocious feature grim with ooze.
> Greater he looks, and more than mortal stares.
>   [325-29]

Yet Father Thames, for all his regality, is overshadowed in the *Dunciad*—like everyone—by Mother Dulness, the presiding counterpart of Anne; Smedley, her subservient priest, is led away into a vacant repose. In one sense the situation repeats that taming of the Thames described in Spenser's lines, a contest between male and female, with female clearly dominant; and Pope's satiric distortion taps a deeper level of response than at first we might imagine. Cities, as Jung and others have argued, in their role as protective enclosures are frequently symbolized in literature as mothers, their rivers interpreted as uniquely feminine, analogous to the pudenda and especially to the power of generation (one further instance of the imposition of human form upon urban space, not merely to organize it, but to give it meaning: Anna Livia Plurabelle in *Finnegans Wake* is an excellent example).[17] The female Augusta in *Windsor-Forest*, astride the Thames as it flows toward ocean and empire, might easily be taken to be an image of powerful maternal creativity served by the river. Undeniably in book II of the *Dunciad* the scene Pope presents is of a vast, mindless, abundant mother overseeing her brood—indeed, her breeding, for the Dunces (who somehow seem in the section Lilliputian) dive in and out of the Fleet's thick waters like spawn, in and out of a "quaking" primal mud. And Virgil's fourth *Eclogue*, which it has been suggested the river games partially ape, is organized by the opposite imagery of sacred motherhood and birth.[18] Other references tend to confirm these impressions of a perverse, destructive maternity:

> Sons of a Day! just buoyant on the flood,
> Then number'd with the puppies in the mud.
> Ask ye their names? I could as soon disclose
> The names of these blind puppies as of those.
> Fast by, like Niobe (her children gone)
> Sits Mother Osborne, stupify'd to stone!

> [307–12]

Mother Osborne, Pope ironically notes, was in fact a man so-called by other Dunces; and for Niobe he cites Ovid's account in the *Metamorphoses*, where she is destroyed by the jealous goddess Latona and turned to stone. But the translator of Homer would not be likely to have forgotten that other, more beautiful version of Niobe's story, which in *Iliad* XXIV Achilles tells to Priam shortly before the first Troy falls.

III

A river of life streams toward its opposite. The exuberance of the games, and their rich allusiveness to distant cities, should not blind us to the seriousness of London's condition. Dulness and her children grotesquely parody the theme of the birth and nurture of a great city, but against these images, deeper still, runs a chill countercurrent. Before he takes on his robe and cassock, Smedley recounts to the Dunces

... how shown him by the Nut-brown maids
A branch of Styx here rises from the Shades,
That tinctur'd as it runs with Lethe's streams,
And wafting Vapours from the Land of dreams,
(As under seas Alphaeus' secret sluice
Bears Pisa's off'rings to his Arethuse)
Pours into Thames: and hence the mingled wave
Intoxicates the pert, and lulls the grave:
Here brisker vapours o'er the Temple creep,
There, all from Paul's to Aldgate drink and sleep.

                                        [337–46]

The underground Styx presses forward ideas appropriate to
the death of Augusta rather than the birth of Dultown: the
river of death, whose fumes lull "the grave" and overcome
both the Temple and St. Paul's, forms another, more ominous
tributary to the Thames. Pope's attention here to images of
dreams and death extends to the repeated word "vapours,"
which belongs to a commonplace eighteenth-century theory
of melancholy and which has its *locus classicus* in Swift's
unnerving account of vaporish madness in *A Tale of a Tub*.[19]
The 1728 version of these lines contains one further case of
numbing inspiration: "And Shadwell nods the poppy on his
brows," explained in a Popean note by the fact that "*Shadwell* took Opium for many years, and died of too large a dose
of it, in the year 1692." In this context we may also think
back to the lines describing Concanen, shortly before Smedley's reappearance:

A cold, long-winded, native of the deep;
If perseverance gain the Diver's prize,
Not everlasting Blackmore this denies:
No noise, no stir, no motion can'st thou make,
Th' unconscious stream sleeps o'er thee like a lake.

                                        [300–304]

"Unconscious" is likely to stand out to a modern reader, re-
inforcing the impression of sleep that is a death, both of
body and mind, a motionless death that neither hears nor
sees. The Twickenham edition quotes a similar use of "un-

conscious" by Thomas Parnell, but more probably Black-more's name is meant to alert us to his earlier multiple use of the word in his epic *Creation* (1712), an ironic opposite to the uncreating *Dunciad.*[20]

Pope's subject here is the death of mind, the death of the city's mind, if we are willing to push the idea of city and body one step further; and all of these scattered images of extinction, gifts of the unpurifying river, are pulled together by Smedley's speech, whose last word "sleep" leads directly into the final event of the heroic games. The reading aloud by College Sophs and Templars drastically enlarges the scope of the satire, spreading the sleep of Dulness irresistibly over the city on similes of wind and water, reaching farther and farther outward in its "all-subduing" work. Another image of polluted water appears.

> As what a Dutchman plumps into the lakes,
> One circle first, and then a second makes;
> What Dulness dropt among her sons imprest
> Like motion from one circle to the rest;
> So from the mid-most the nutation spreads
> Round and more round, o'er all the sea of heads.
>
> [405–10]

And then this sea is replaced in the last quatrain by the original images of sewer, Fleet Ditch, and unconsciousness:

> How Henley lay inspir'd beside a sink
> And to mere mortals seem'd a Priest in drink:
> While others, timely, to the neighb'ring Fleet
> (Haunt of the Muses) made their safe retreat.
>
> [425–28]

Here the action of the original *Dunciad* ended, leaving its hero alone to be transported to an underworld of dreams while London slept.

IV

"Beauty, cleanliness, and order," Freud remarks, "obviously occupy a special position among the requirements of civiliza-

tion."[21] There is one additional analogue for Pope's Fleet
Ditch: the Cloaca Maxima of ancient Rome, an infamous
gutter that ran from the Forum to the Tiber and through the
satires of Juvenal and Plautus. Pope's mock-heroic framework
and the strange beauty of much of his language obscure to
some degree the fact that, metaphorically and authentically,
he is talking about a sewer. The "sink" beside which Henley
snores was a common name for the open kennels (from OF
canal) that flowed along the center of eighteenth-century
London streets, signs of the city's corruption unavoidably
underfoot for everyone (moreover, "sink" was sometimes
used to name the lower organs of the body).[22] Pope's rather
lyrical diction in these circumstances is perhaps deliberate,
for two friends and literary allies, Swift and Gay, had earlier
written respectively briefer and greater poems of London
sanitation in the same burlesque style. It is worth pausing for
a moment to observe their separate courses.

Swift's mock-georgic "Description of a City Shower" begins with one sign of a coming storm:

> Returning Home at Night, you'll find the Sink
> Strike your offended Sense with double Stink.[23]

And proceeds to set London awash in every kind of liquid,
from wine to coffee to liquor to spleen, until the "shower"
of the title swells into a "Flood" and a "Deluge." We may
discover wonderfully diminished versions of familiar images
here: the maternal symbolism of city and river, for example,
becomes "Brisk *Susan*" hauling in the laundry and then

> . . . that Sprinkling which some careless Quean
> Flirts on you from her Mop, but not so clean.

City commerce is reduced to "dagled Females" crowding into
shops to pretend to bargain; the dangers of urban life are
ludicrously imaged in the Beau "Box'd" in a sedan chair who
trembles at the sound of rain on his roof, just as the Greeks
at Troy listened to Laocoon hammer against the wooden
horse. And the Beau's predicament along with the entrap-
ment of other citizens in shops, sheds, doorways contributes
to a feeling of *imprisonment* in the town as well as of dirt

and danger. (A similar feeling is present in Swift's shorter London poem, "A Description of the Morning" with its turnkeys and prisoners. Curiously, Hogarth, although we think of him as expert in portraying the vigorous bustle of London life, communicates the same insistent sense of enclosure in his crowded theaters, streets, and prisons.) But the most-quoted section of the poem, its conclusion, goes beyond such civilized cleverness and releases a measure of that dim unease Swift almost always causes:

NOW from all Parts the swelling Kennels flow,
And bear their *Trophies* with them as they go:
Filth of all Hues and Odours seem to tell
What Streets they sail'd from, by the Sight and Smell.
They, as each Torrent drives, with rapid Force
From *Smithfield,* or St. *Pulchre*'s shape their Course,
And in huge Confluent join at *Snow-Hill* Ridge,
Fall from the *Conduit* prone to *Holborn-Bridge.*
Sweepings from Butchers Stalls, Dung, Guts, and Blood,
Drown'd Puppies, stinking Sprats, all drench'd in Mud,
Dead Cats and Turnip-Tops come tumbling down the Flood.

These are not Pope's still ditches and ironic tributaries, where Dunces float and paddle. Swift's rainstorm billows with motion, energy; its waters swell and flow, its torrents drive "with rapid Force," and rush together "in huge Confluent" just above Holborn Bridge, where Fleet Ditch begins. In contrast with the gentle waves of sleep that cover the Dunces' nodding heads, Swift's deluge tears away the solid evidence of the city's filth and tumbles it toward the reader in a crest of debris. Martin Price observes that the randomness of the kennel seems to match the randomness of human association in the city ("Here various Kinds by various Fortunes led,/ Commence Acquaintance underneath a Shed").[24] But these amusing incoherences are still more closely associated with the randomness of battle. Impending storms in Virgil's first *Georgic* prophesy catastrophic war, and virtually every classical and biblical allusion of the poem recalls the doom of a great city—Troy, Rome by conquest, Jerusalem by flood. Swift's kennels overflow like a mighty river, seize "Trophies"

like an army, and swirl like the insane stream Eridanus of
Georgic I around the sheep and cattle markets on Snow Hill
(the "Dung, Guts, and Blood" of line 61). From thence they
roll their slaughter past either Smithfield, site of Bartholomew Fair, or past St. Sepulchre's church, where the great bell
tolled for prisoners on their way from neighboring Newgate
prison to the hangman at Tyburn. If Swift's purpose was to
describe the purification of London, its washing clean by
heaven, his effect is nevertheless to drown it. He leaves us
at midpoint in a rising flood, a formless, undifferentiated flux
of objects neither purified nor restored to order, an image of
sinful chaos Virgilian in origin but Swiftian in disgust.

Trivia often gives the same impression of a London at sea,
waterlogged and sinking, but Gay's gentle voice, though it
reaches the highest ranges of mock-heroic, celebrates the
London scene with an affection we miss in the brisker intelli-
gences of Swift and Pope.[25]

> But when the Swinging signs your ears offend
> With creaking noise, then rainy floods impend;
> Soon shall the kennels swell with rapid streams,
> And rush in muddy torrents to the *Thames*. . . .
> Church-monuments foretell the changing air;
> Then *Niobe* dissolves into a tear
> And sweats with secret grief: you'll hear the sounds
> Of whistling winds, e'er kennels break their bounds;
> Ungrateful odours common-shores diffuse,
> And dropping vaults distill unwholesome dews,
> E'er the tiles rattle with the smoaking show'r,
> And spouts on men their torrents pour.
>
> [I, 157–74]

To a far greater extent than Pope's or Swift's, Gay's London
is a purely literary artifact. Our experience of it is filtered
almost entirely through allusions, recollections, imitations—
of Virgil, Juvenal, Dryden—and the emotions generated are of
urbane pleasure in its impressions, satisfaction in its surfaces,
as if the London Spy had been refined into a connoisseur.
Gay confessed that he owed several hints for the poem to
Swift, yet his indebtedness is for tactics, not strategy. His

muddy torrents lack a specific direction, his Niobe a human urban counterpart. The energetic soaking he gives London never places the city in danger; his classical allusions never cohere into a pattern. For all its charming mockery, in short, *Trivia* describes no satiric city. Remembering the anger that transforms the rivers and streets of the *Dunciad* or "A City Shower," we may be struck by how often the Augustan satirists harness disparate images in a kind of zeugmatic plot: give two subjects to a single action, as Pope equates the progress of Dulness and the progress of Aeneas, as Swift equates the preaching of madmen and enthusiasts in *A Tale of a Tub,* as Gay himself equates the thievery of highwaymen and statesmen in *The Beggar's Opera.* It is a rhetorical trick that reveals a consistent, ironic, condensing habit of mind. But *Trivia* is innocent of any such plot. As he takes up the ancient images of city and river, Gay's temperament remains genially, even stubbornly nonapocalyptic, and in his hands they recall but do not release the destructive rivers of earlier cities. For once the Augustan mode is unanxious, content with its inheritance. This London is linked (but not bound) to a solemn past by the slenderest possible threads of allusion.[26]

V

The theater appears prominently—one would like to say takes a prominent role—in almost every account of eighteenth-century London. Few novels of the period fail to include an evening at the theater in their London setting, like those in *Tom Jones* and *Roderick Random;* James Thomson makes it the heart of London in *Winter;* and no guidebook or satiric tour was complete without a description of the allures of the Drury Lane playhouse, directed by the Dunce Colley Cibber, or the marginally more respectable Theatre Royal in nearby Haymarket (at various times four other theaters were in operation, notably one at Lincoln's Inn Fields). Most descriptions, like this irresistible account from the *Spectator* (240), seize upon the uproarious behavior of the audience:

> This was a very lusty Fellow, but withal a sort of Beau, who getting into one of the Side-Boxes on the Stage before the Curtain drew, was disposed to shew the whole

Audience his Activity by leaping over the Spikes; he pass'd from thence to one of the ent'ring Doors, where he took Snuff with a tolerable good Grace, display'd his fine Cloaths, made two or three feint Passes at the Curtain with his Cane, then faced about and appear'd at t'other Door: Here he affected to survey the whole House, bow'd and smil'd at Random, and then shew'd his Teeth (which were some of them indeed very white): After this he retir'd behind the Curtain, and obliged us with several Views of his Person from every Opening.[27]

Others raise the theater into London's equivalent of the Roman circus, stressing not only its licentious plays but also its promiscuous mingling of all classes, from the footmen who sat jeering in the highest balcony to the dissolute nobility and orange girls (prostitutes) who wandered the pit. A social melting pot, not infrequently at a boil—no season was complete without a riot, thought Horace Walpole—the theaters were London landmarks as much as St. Paul's or the Tower Zoo. "Perhaps you might expect mighty matters from the *Playhouse* too," the author of *Tricks of the Town* writes to a country friend; "why, indeed, that is the only Diversion we have in Town, that can any ways pretend to a Singularity, or Exception from the Country"; and he goes on to devote two lengthy, interested letters to the theater's offenses.[28]

These elements of sensuality and abandon are centrally identified in many minds with the very nature of the city and tend to undercut its mythic pretensions. The emphasis urban life gives to external appearances, for example—to clothes, coaches, servants—is matched by the theater's fondness for costume and spectacle, for "the long-applauding note," as Pope writes, that greets "Quin's high plume, or Oldfield's petticoat."[29] And the costumes belong to a still more troubling aspect of the playhouse that urban life reflects: the temptation to shed old identities and toy with new ones, just as actors do. Anyone who has ever plunged into a metropolis such as London was becoming has felt this temptation, this opportunity for forbidden change and for release from strict sincerity; it is an inevitable function of the city's anonymity and dependence upon externalities in personal relationships. In some cases the metamorphoses are merely comic. No one, for example, has ever caved in more wholeheartedly than Boswell, who in his *London Journal* attempts to form his character by stagecraft, and rolls about the city from playhouse to actress to surgeon in the part of Macheath, exploiting to the fullest the theater's urbane possibilities for liberation. But taken far enough such liberation grows ominous, as Moll Flanders in her numerous disguises seems to suggest. Rousseau sees the theater as analogue for Parisian hypocrisy.[30] Jane Austen's *Mansfield Park,* a novel that openly pits rural values against London corruption, makes a scene of amateur theatricals into a clear symbol of the threat posed by the city to the stability of both community and selfhood. Again, public masquerades, popular in London throughout the first half of the century, were frequently attacked by contemporary moralists for encouragement of libidinous "Assignations and Intrigues," and even briefly closed by royal order. "The Misfortune of the thing," according to the *Spectator* (14), "is, that People dress themselves in what they have a mind to be, and not what they are fit for." The obvious link with theater is underscored by their presence in the Haymarket Opera House, sponsored by notorious impresario John Heidegger. And the recurrent references to Proteus in the *Dunciad* also carry us rapidly toward images of theater, masquerade, and then, as A. Bartlett Giamatti has eloquently demonstrated, toward the destruction of great cities that Proteus, who destroys as well as builds, often causes.[31]

The first lines of the *Dunciad* yoke Dultown and the contemporary theater:

> The Mighty Mother, and her Son who brings
> The Smithfield Muses to the ear of Kings,
> I sing.

Explained in a topographical note: "*Smithfield* is the place where Bartholomew Fair was kept, whose shews, machines, and dramatical entertainments, formerly agreeable only to the taste of the Rabble were by the Hero of this poem, and others of equal genius, brought to the Theatres of Covent-Garden, Lincolns-Inn-Fields, and the Hay-market to be the reigning pleasures of the Court and Town." Pope's note could serve as a précis for the progress of Dulness, the encroachment of the boisterous, anarchic "theater" of Smithfield upon both the middle-class and polite tastes. He takes the theater, indeed, as loose synecdoche for decaying London, presenting them as greater and smaller stages for disorder

> 'Till rais'd from booths, to Theatre, to Court,
> Her seat imperial Dulness shall transport.
>   [III, 299–300]

At the same time, Pope is also drawing for his satire upon the traditional idea of the theater as a microcosm of human life, a conservative idea that stresses the need for every actor to accept unhesitatingly his appointed role; to act otherwise, as Aubrey Williams says, "to shed one role for another, is 'pride' or 'presumption,' while the effect is to bring confusion into God's ordered plan, to spoil the play of life for the other actors."[32] The Dunces, of course, exhibit exactly such disordering pride, generally in their attempts to claim too much for themselves, specifically in their astonishing practices upon the London stage. The nature of the offense is most clearly seen in the elaborate parody of actual Cibberian spectacles in book III, where somber intimations of Isaiah and Revelation in the battle of "Contending Theatres"—Drury Lane and Lincoln's Inn—partly counterbalance Pope's satiric glee. Advancing technical resources for theatrical effect in the early eighteenth century produced a fascination with special effects—machines for making thunder, for example, such as John Dennis invented—and the result was often a literal mechanization of the spirit: gigantic extravaganzas of sound and light that substitute sensation (or conflagration) for drama.

> Hell rises, Heav'n descends, and dance on Earth:
> Gods, imps, and monsters, music, rage, and mirth,
> A fire, a jigg, a battle, and a ball,
> 'Till one wide conflagration swallows all.

> Thence a new world to Nature's laws unknown,
> Breaks out refulgent, with a heav'n its own:
> Another Cynthia her new journey runs,
> And other planets circle other suns.
> The forests dance, the rivers upward rise,
> Whales sport in woods, and dolphins in the skies;
> And last, to give the whole creation grace,
> Lo! one vast Egg produces human race.
>   [III, 237–48]

"This monstrous absurdity" of a rising Hell and a descending heavenly backdrop, Pope declares in a note, "was actually represented in Tibbald's Rape of Proserpine"; and in the same farce "a corn-field was set on fire: whereupon the other playhouse had a barn burnt down for the recreation of the spectators." Worse yet, Harlequin (played by John Rich) was actually hatched from an enormous plaster egg on stage, to universal admiration; and the atmosphere of impiety was heightened, as Williams notes, by Rich's trick of attaching tinsel stars and suns on stage "to parody the original creation of the heavenly lights."[33]

These excesses are joined to the city at this point by the apparition of Elkanah Settle, who locates the source of Dulness's contagion squarely within "Lud's old walls," where he began as elected City Poet (but confesses that he ended his days keeping a booth in Bartholomew Fair, acting the part of a green leather dragon). At last even the theme of unnatural birth takes on theatrical guise:

> Another AEschylus appears! prepare
> For new abortions, all ye pregnant fair!
> In flames, like Semele's, be brought to bed,
> While op'ning Hell spouts wild-fire at your head.
>   [III, 314–16]

And a variation occurs in "BAY's monster-breeding breast;/ Bays, formed by nature Stage and Town to bless" (I, 108–09). But if this monstrous garishness alarms Pope, in the end it is the acceptance, by those who should know better, of Smithfield theater that draws his greatest anger, in part because the standards of English drama seemed to dissolve at Cibber's touch (they had stiffened to absurdity, Pope believed, with the 1728 hero Lewis Theobald, editor of Shakespeare); in part because Cibber's success represented a further step in the ascendancy of city tradesmen over gentlemen. The audience that lolled lazy and corrupt in its chairs was as complicit as the hack authors who diverted them.

Pope's attacks on London theater are supported by other Tory satirists—Swift, for example, skewers its pretensions in "A Letter to a Young Poet"—but nowhere outside of the *Dunciad* is the link between city and theater clearer than in the concluding chapter of *Peri Bathous*, "A Project for the Advancement of the Stage," a Scriblerian production probably written by Pope. The project is no less than city building: Pope proposes that London's two chief theaters "be incorporated into one Company," along with the Royal Academy of Music and a troupe of prize fighters, and be lodged in

> a spacious Building . . . erected at the Public expense, capable of containing at least *ten thousand* Spectators, which is become absolutely necessary by the great addition of Children and Nurses to the Audience, since the new Entertainments. That there be a Stage as large as the Athenian, which was near ninety thousand geometrical paces square, and separate divisions for the two Houses of Parliament, my Lords the Judges, the honourable Directors of the Academy, and Court of Aldermen, who shall all have their Places frank.[34]

He wistfully hopes that Westminster Hall may be given over for this purpose; that failing, "it is left to the wisdom of the Nation whether *Somerset House* may not be demolished, and a Theatre built upon that site." Pope's ambitions do not stop with this merely literal replacement of the existing London by its dramatic shadow: in the wings are even more elaborate schemes for the government of this new city, with councils of critics, networks of transportation (along the Thames), provisions "to prevent unmarried Actresses making away with their Infants," and finally a merger of the king's

Privy Council and the theater's government. London, if not
all the world, is to become a stage for Cibber's Dulness. Not
until Great Anarch—formerly Great Anna—lets fall her curtain will the identification of bad theater and reprobate city
be plainer.

VI

"What was said of Rome, adorned by Augustus, may be
applied by an easy metaphor to English poetry embellished
by Dryden, 'lateritiam invenit, marmoream reliquit,' he found
it brick, and he left it marble."[35] Johnson states plainly, as
always, a connection often felt but rarely acknowledged between city and language: few instances in eighteenth-century
literature spell out the analogy exactly, yet in the case of
London, at least, its pressures recur insistently everywhere.
Discussion, brief or extended, of shop signs, street cries,
coffeehouse gossip, boatmen's obscenity, tradesmen's blunt-
ness, city slang, fashionable argot, like the critical example of
Rome all help to demarcate the city's role as arbiter of talk.
At the same time they remind us that language itself is our
greatest collective activity, our unmistakably human way of
creating community, the city we live in.

Insofar as it organizes ourselves and our experience into
coherence, language excludes chaos as firmly as any mythical
city walls *in illo tempore;* but of course the language that
brings men together in cities also drives them apart sometimes, as urban crowding increases the randomness of what is
said and heard, as the noise of mobs and small talk drowns or
empties language of its meaning. (*The World* 102 [1754]
tackles the problem forthrightly: "In order . . . to interpret
every new word, and what is still more important, to give the
different acceptations of the same words, according to the
various senses in which they are received and understood in
the different parts of this extensive metropolis, I would
recommend a small portable vocabulary to be annually published and bound up with the almanack.") We can see both
possibilities in a single image like the Stock Exchange, that
ubiquitous symbol of London which serves Defoe, Addison,

and Voltaire as a model of harmonious language, a benign
Babel or literal discors concordia. "There is no Place in the
Town which I so much love to frequent as the *Royal-
Exchange,*" Addison writes; ". . . I am infinitely delighted
in mixing with these several Ministers of Commerce, as they
are distinguished by their different Walks and different
Languages: Sometimes I am justled among a Body of *Armeni-
ans:* Sometimes I am lost in a Crowd of *Jews;* and sometimes
make one in a Groupe of *Dutch-men.*"³⁶ Others, less moved
by London's commercial greatness, treat the same scene ir-
reverently: "'Tis a vast heap of Stones, and the confusion of
Languages makes it resemble *Babel.* The Noise in it is like
that of Bees; a strange Humming or Buzzing, of walking
tongues and feet; it is a kind of still Roaring, or loud Whis-
per."³⁷ Shop signs, for which London was famous, can create
a similar ambiguity: to the characters in *The Country Wife*
they are fine new sights, a reason to tour the city, while the
Tatler (18) complains that their illiteracy misleads more than
informs, and often causes him to lose his way. Gay hears the
street cries of London as music, signaling order as songbirds
do:

> Successive crys the seasons' change declare,
> And mark the monthly progress of the year.
> Hark, how the streets with treble voices ring,
> To sell the bounteous product of the spring!
>
> [*Trivia,* II, 425–28]

But to Addison in the *Spectator* (251) they emblematize the
disorder of London life, its uncommunicating individualism:

> Vocal Cries are of much larger Extent, and indeed so full
> of Incongruities and Barbarism, that we appear a distracted
> City to Foreigners, who do not comprehend the Meaning
> of such Enormous Outcries. Milk is generally sold in a
> Note above *Elah,* and in Sounds so exceeding shrill, that
> it often sets our Teeth on edge. The Chimney Sweeper
> is confined to no certain pitch; he sometimes utters him-
> self in the deepest Base, and sometimes in the sharpest
> Treble; sometimes in the highest, and sometimes in the
> lowest Note of the Gamut. . . .

I must not here omit one particular Absurdity which runs through this whole Vociferous Generation, and which renders their Cries very often not only incommodious, but altogether useless to the Publick, I mean that Idle Accomplishment which they all of them aim at, of Crying so as not to be understood.

Although Addison speaks lightly of this cacophony, he is nonetheless touching upon a theme that sets in motion much of Augustan satire, the clash between true and false language. His good-natured plan for tuning the music of the London streets joins him to Swift and Pope and every other satirist—like Orwell and Pound in our own time—who takes style as an index of civilization.

In the *Dunciad* Pope distinguishes two kinds of false language, chaotic or corrupt, and associates them both with the great city that makes and unmakes them. Chaotic language, moreover, also appears in two separate guises, the first of which arises very early in the poem in a complicated context of Miltonic allusion, theater, and mob:

> Here she beholds the Chaos dark and deep,
> Where nameless Somethings in their causes sleep,
> 'Till genial Jacob, or a warm Third day,
> Call forth each mass, a Poem, or a Play:
> How hints, like spawn, scarce quick in embryo lie,
> How new-born nonsense first is taught to cry,
> Maggots half-form'd in rhyme exactly meet,
> And learn to crawl upon poetic feet.
> Here one poor word an hundred clenches makes,
> And ductile dulness new meanders takes;
> There motley Images her fancy strike,
> Figures ill pair'd, and Similes unlike.
> She sees a Mob of Metaphors advance,
> Pleas'd with the madness of the mazy dance.
>
> [I, 55–67]

This is a creation scene. Both the theater ("a warm Third day," when playwrights received the proceeds of the house) and publishers ("genial Jacob" Tonson) serve here as suns, warming the unnamed, unfocused substances of language into monstrous life; the word "causes" in line 56 has a technical philosophical meaning, too, as Pope must have known, probably alluding to the second of Aristotle's four causes, the formal, which may be translated into Greek as *logos,* the creating word. Consistent with its activity of spreading and expanding, the language born here has an unresolved, disruptive quality, like the Protean bards mentioned a few lines earlier who "Escape in Monsters, and amaze the town" (38). "The effect of these Protean hacks," writes A. Bartlett Giamatti, "is to 'amaze the town,' that is, by their writing to introduce into the human community a kind of confusion which finally reduces the city to chaotic wilderness."[38] This chaotic language, with its theological resonance, its freakish distortions, clearly repels Pope and his reader. Another version of such formlessness, the infantile noise of the Dunces at play in book II, seems far less ominous—and indeed, Emrys Jones suggests that Pope is drawn to their cheerful, preliterate chatter and finds it attractive:

> Now turn to diff'rent sports (the Goddess cries)
> And learn, my sons, the wond'rous pow'r of Noise.
> To move, to raise, to ravish ev'ry heart,
> With Shakespear's nature, or with Johnson's art,
> Let others aim: 'Tis yours to shake the soul
> With Thunder rumbling from the mustard bowl,
> With horns and trumpets now to madness swell,
> Now sink in sorrows with a tolling bell;
> Such happy arts attention can command,
> When fancy flags, and sense is at a stand.
>
> [II, 221–30]

This chaos also levels all distinctions, but like the street noises of London, it has a vigor, a release about it, that charms us, like schoolchildren's shouts or Swift's baby talk to Stella. The similes of animals that follow this passage— "Monkey-mimics," "Cat-calls"—culminate in a long description of Dissenting Asses whose "Harmonic twang" sounds all over London:

> But far o'er all, sonorous Blackmore's strain;
> Walls, steeples, skies, bray back to him again.

In Tot'nam fields, the brethren, with amaze,
Prick all their ears up, and forget to graze;
Long Chanc'ry-lane retentive rolls the sound,
And courts to courts return it round and round;
Thames wafts it thence to Rufus' roaring hall,
And Hungerford re-echoes bawl for bawl.

[II, 259–66]

Aubrey Williams has shown how the places named here carefully delimit the boundaries of Westminster, the polite fron-
tiers of advancing Dultown (we can add that the courts along
Chancery Lane, Rufus's Houses of Parliament, and Hungerford
Market are *already* scenes of infected language); and Pope's
own note quotes a Virgilian echo, the sounding of Alecto's
horn that precedes the battle for Latium.[39] The "amaze" of
line 261 shares the dark shading of its earlier Protean usage:
we feel the sportive quality of Blackmore's bray surrendering
to the undertones of civic struggle and defeat that are the
Dunciad's real concern.

The speech of animals and Dunces—all the more appropriate when we recall the many eighteenth-century comparisons
of London to a wild forest—reaches the shrill pitch of torture
in book III, where it presumes to appear in literature as well
as games:

Some strain in rhyme; the Muses, on their racks,
Scream like the winding of ten thousand jacks:
Some free from rhyme or reason, rule or check,
Break Priscian's head, and Pegasus's neck. . . .
  Silence, ye Wolves! while Ralph to Cynthia howls,
And makes Night hideous—Answer him, ye Owls!
  Sense, speech, and measure, living tongues and dead,
Let all give way—and Morris may be read.

[III, 159–68]

And this painful chaos of language attains its full, thunderous
volume in the Italian opera that had lately captivated the
London stage and that Pope and others found so distasteful.
In its last moments all meaningful language is compressed
into a single sound, an irresistible, unending trill:

O *Cara! Cara!* silence all that train:
Joy to great Chaos! Let Division reign:
Chromatic tortures soon shall drive them hence,
Break all their nerves, and fritter all their sense:
One Trill shall harmonize joy, grief, and rage,
Wake the dull Church, and lull the ranting Stage.

[IV, 53–58]

VII

Chaotic language, whether infantile or simply confused, whether brightened by a warm third day or obscured by universal darkness, frames the far more extensive presentation of corrupt language in the *Dunciad,* in which deterioration rather than disorder is Pope's theme. The grinding effect of commercial values on literature, for example, has already been mentioned, whereby the laws of supply and demand, not excellence, determine success, and plays and poems are sold by bulk, like dry goods, to a clientele of housewives, butchers, and apprentices. Hence the eastern end of the Strand, in the early part of the century chief site of booksellers and publishers like the unspeakable Curll, is the scene of the mock-heroic games of book II and forms an avenue (or beachhead), both real and metaphorical, for the invasion of Westminster by Grub Street. Thanks to their pandering enterprise, as Pope saw it, pamphlets, piracies, fripperies were smothering the standards of a former age, crowding out genuine writers from what had become merely a market. Or again, the London theater, whose ultimate fate of unintelligibility was foreshadowed in opera, likewise played to the mobs. Pope's description of the "many-headed Monster of the Pit" goes on to show how garish spectacle, appealing only to childish taste, replaces language:

The Play stands still; damn action and discourse,
Back fly the scenes, and enter foot and horse. . . .
Ah luckless Poet! stretch thy lungs and roar,
That Bear or Elephant shall heed thee more;
While all its throats the Gallery extends,
And all the Thunder of the Pit ascends!

> Loud as the Wolves, on Orcas' stormy steep,
> Howl to the roarings of the Northern deep . . .
> Booth enters—hark! the Universal peal!
> "But has he spoken?" Not a syllable.
> > [*Imitations of Horace,* Ep. I, ii, 314 ff.]

Here discourse passes rapidly through all stages of corruption, from human roars to lupine howls to the absolute silence of Booth, and carries downward with it not only the whores and apprentices who throng the playhouse, but also the Lords and Ladies who have unlearned their heritage.

Impermanence of language in the *Dunciad* is paralleled by the impermanence of cities. Pope seems to have concerned himself often about the stability of English—an eloquent exchange of letters shows Bolingbroke urging him to write only in English and thus preserve and fix it—and like Swift (and Johnson afterward) to have responded sensitively to its changing, not to say collapsing nature.[40] His concern is for English, as we feel in his imitations of Chaucer, Donne, and Spenser (and his parody of archaic language in *Dunciad* III, 185–90); but as translator and classicist he extends it instinctively to the ancient languages. Book IV details their humiliation at the hands of ponderous editors:

> Roman and Greek Grammarians! know your Better:
> Author of something yet more great than Letter;
> While tow'ring o'er your Alphabet, like Saul,
> Stands our Digamma, and o'er-tops them all.
> > [IV, 215–18]

And Augustan Gradgrinds teach only classical words, divorcing them from meaning and strapping them like dead weight across their students' memories:

> We ply the Memory, we load the brain,
> Bind rebel Wit, and double chain on chain,
> Confine the thought, to exercise the breath;
> And keep them in the pale of Words till death.
> > [IV, 157–60]

These and dozens of other instances of diminution are linked

again and again to the great cities of Rome and Troy, para-
digms for modern Augusta, whose physical destruction is
now being imitated in the languages they nourished. The traditional comparison of architecture and literature, which presents poems as buildings, takes on a special poignance in the
Dunciad as Pope anchors it in London reality:

> See under Ripley rise a new White-hall,
> While Jones' and Boyle's united labours fall:
> While Wren with sorrow to the grave descends,
> Gay dies unpension'd with a hundred friends.
> Hibernian Politics, O Swift! thy fate;
> And Pope's, ten years to comment and translate.
>
> [III, 327–32]

The architectural monuments that he laments, the very opposite of Dulness's "sacred Dome," belong to a whole cluster of
images of collapsing monuments in books III and IV; and
Pope's verse leaves us sharply aware of the double sense of
"monument,"—"speaking monuments" in Wordsworth's
phrase—structures in both stones and words that are liable to
reworking or decay.[41] Swift contradicts Horace, wishfully,
by declaring that "all new, affected Modes of Speech, whether
borrowed from the Court, the Town, or the Theatre, are the
first perishing Parts in any Language."[42] The Roman poet
had said in a moving passage of *Ars poetica* that the earliest
words in a language, not the latest, drop off like the leaves
of the forest. But both Pope and Swift understand the newest
words to be agents of Dulness, creations of the fashionable
life of the town, enemies of that clear imagination which the
ancient standards represented and inspire. The elegiac note
sticks in their throats. Their emblem of language, like their
emblem of an abiding community, exists apart from the
processes of time. "The grass withereth, the flower fadeth,"
say the Scriptures in a passage Pope knew: "but the word of
our God shall stand forever" (Isaiah 40:8).

   The themes of corrupted language and corrupted city come
together most completely in the concluding lines of book I of
the *Dunciad,* when Mother Dulness crowns the chosen Cibber:

> She ceas'd. Then swells the Chapel-royal throat:
> God save king Cibber! mounts in ev'ry note.
> Familiar White's, God save king Colley! cries;
> God save king Colley! Drury-lane replies:
> To Needham's quick the voice triumphal rode,
> But pious Needham dropt the name of God;
> Back to the Devil the last echoes roll,
> And Coll! each Butcher roars at Hockley-hole.
>
> [319–26]

Here the traditional formula "God save the king" visibly, audibly diminishes with each repetition, until the butchers of Hockley Hole reduce it to an uncreating syllable: "Coll!" At the same time each repetition moves across the face of London, from its western to eastern edges, and also from the "Chapel-royal" to the "Devil," a tavern in Fleet Street, touching such inevitable landmarks of language along the way as chocolate houses ("Familiar White's") and theaters (Drury Lane). And the last lines of the book complete the transformation of human to animal language, alluding scornfully to the foolish frogs in Aesop who misunderstand and pervert the ritual phrase: "And the hoarse nation croak'd, God save King Log!" "Pious Needham," whose "quick" may remind us of the "quick in embryo" of I, 76, was more commonly known in London as Mother Needham, a madam noted both for enterprise and bad language; she appears in the first plate of Hogarth's *Harlot's Progress*, welcoming the country girl to London. Her profanity, recurring form of urban corruption in the *Dunciad*, emerges a few lines earlier:

> Let Bawdry, Bilingsgate, my daughters dear
> Support his front, and Oaths bring up the rear.
>
> [307–08]⁴³

And the idea of perverse motherhood that she represents, an idea deeply joined to the idea of a city as we have seen, figures in Dulness's complaints of infertility:

> O! when shall rise a Monarch all our own,
> And I, a Nursing-mother, rock the throne,

'Twixt Prince and People close the Curtain draw,
Shade him from Light, and cover him from Law;
Fatten the Courtier, starve the learned band,
And suckle Armies, and dry-nurse the land:
'Till Senates nod to Lullabies divine,
And all be sleep, as at an Ode of thine.

[311–18]

The motif of childish language so characteristic of the Dunces at play in the streets is adumbrated here, as are the motifs of sleep and unconsciousness in "Lullabies" and the rocking throne; the emphasis on nursing and suckling in these lines may also suggest to us the orality of language itself—of mother tongues—though frustrated Dulness, we realize, true to her own sterility, hopes only to "dry-nurse the land."

The fate of language is the fate of the city. This entire section in book I, added only in the 1743 edition, distinctly echoes the apocalyptic conclusion of book IV, with its thrones, darkness, mighty mother, and blasted language. So pervasive, indeed, is Pope's theme that many readers will think ahead to a similar disintegration in modern literature, the "Oxen of the Sun" chapter of Joyce's *Ulysses,* where a glorious inheritance of English gives way at last to an all-conquering urban vulgarity: an incoherent, ungrammatical babble of faded blasphemy and advertising jingles.

The comparison of Pope and Joyce reminds us that both were authors of mock-epics rather than epics, and that much of their mockery springs from the contrast they never cease to feel between the real cities their heroes wander, dear and dirty, dear and distracting, and the ideal cities they imagine too well.[44] But "contrast" may be too cautious a word. The *Dunciad* is in its deepest moments about failure. Not simply the failure of the outward world, of pastoral or urban land-scapes, to obey the pressures of ideals, but finally the failure of self to sustain self, to answer its own promises. We need hardly invoke the familiar psychological proposition that great satirists always include themselves in their attack, though one feels its presence in the *Dunciad,* as the satire ex-pands in the fourth book and lights go out one by one across

Pope's vision. The sense of failure, personal and universal, that pervades Pope's later poetry springs from comparison, as all such judgments do, comparison between the certainties possessed in the *Pastorals* and *Windsor-Forest* and the loss of them in the satires of the 1730s and the final *Dunciad.* For some loss there is, as Wordsworth believed, abundant recompense. Memory, new powers, the "sense sublime/Of something far more deeply interfused." Yet as surely as the Blatant Beast will return again and again and again to Spenser's blighted pastoral, so will Pope's version of it, the spreading plague of Dulness, bring down those glittering towers and spoil those enameled gardens with which, so long ago, he began. Should we not say that epic requires unreal cities, mythical, at a distance from time and from too close inspection? Troy, Athens, Cleopolis, Rome: the epic masters the processes of human time by linking generation to generation, pointing forward with pater Anchises toward some final symbol of enduring community, or backward with Aeneas toward some shattered image of it which explains the present; but these are always distant cities, in time and place. Pope's London in certain senses has simply grown too real—too vast, too full of problems, too insistently itself—to serve as epic symbol any longer. Like Defoe, he experiences London as an external force, a thing with energy and destiny of its own, inhuman, beyond his power to order, a mill grinding down slowly the walls of Augusta. The dreamlike quality of Defoe's *Journal of the Plague Year* is not absent from the *Dunciad,* whose confusing, theatrical fantasies are often described as surreal; and more than one reader has felt the trancelike effect of Wordsworth's vision of London in *The Prelude.* The city is too much with them. Their humanizing dreams are ways of escape from a pressing, unchecked reality.

3

The Happy Valley
and Its Discontents

In the early fall of 1764 Boswell, then twenty-four and studying law for a season in Holland, asked Sir David Dalrymple to intercede with his father and arrange the conditions of his return to Scotland. Sir David's reply cannot have scattered his young friend's gloom. "To stipulate that you should go annually to London," he wrote, "whether you have anything to do there or not—if you were my son, I would as soon agree to your making an annual jaunt to Sodom and Gomorrah, where though iron swims, feathers sink."[1]

No doubt Sir David meant to describe London as an unnatural place, a topsy-turvy inversion of everything normal and fitting, but he may also have been alluding to the fate of character in the city, to the iron-souled personality who navigates it and the light-headed soul who disappears in its tides in an instant. He would already have had ample reason to doubt Boswell's buoyancy. A three-month trip to London in 1760, intended to distract him from a flirtation with Roman Catholicism, had been followed by a nine-month stay in 1762–63 while Boswell, now legally of age but dependent upon his father for funds, had angled for a commission in the Royal Footguards. Instead, both trips had opened new vistas of debauchery, enriching the brothels and surgeries of the metropolis and permanently turning Boswell's eyes toward the dazzle of town life.

Like almost everything he did, Boswell's London excesses had their literary models. (Dalrymple remarked that he had gotten his scheme from *Tristram Shandy*.) The *London Journal* revolves like a carousel through an irreconcilable set of exemplars from early eighteenth-century literature: Addison, a sobering figure of dignified urbanity, Macheath of *The Beggar's Opera*, Sir John Brute from Vanbrugh's *Provoked Wife*, even the unlucky heroes of a boyhood favorite, *The Lives of the Convicts*, all serve as guides in his new freedom.[2] But the path Sir David feared Boswell would travel had grimmer prototypes. "The Rake's Progress" was a staple of London mythology long before Hogarth engraved his famous series in 1735. Fictional characters like Richardson's Lovelace and real-life reprobates like Francis Charteris (the "Rape-Master General of Great Britain") and the earl of Rochester had made familiar the trajectory of vice: from drunkenness, gaming, women, a libertine was launched like a Roman candle on a dreadful course toward obliteration in a Newgate or a Bedlam cell.[3] Their careers were continual sermons for wayward youth, warnings as dramatically present to the popular consciousness as the moldering heads of Jacobite rebels still piked above Temple Bar. The complex and uniform fate of the rake during this period, moreover, suggests that in one further way the traditional figure of the adventurer was becoming urbanized. For as it reduces the scale of action, from sailing ships to sedan chairs, from kingdoms to parishes, the city intensifies the literary possibilities of such a character. In its dense atmosphere of secrecy and freedom he paces restlessly between established categories—the taut beau of Restoration comedy, whose sexuality grows monotonous as well as humorous; the Macheath of Newgate pastoral; the sulphurous Richardsonian tyrant of prostitutes and virgins—and his obsession takes on a psychological and even tragic interest.

I

The perils of this moral descent through London are nowhere more striking than in a chronicler of urban folly whom

Boswell firmly admired and whom, along with Sterne, he
may well have tried to imitate in his journals. Mr. Wilson's
tale in *Joseph Andrews* (III, iii)—often thought to be autobio-
graphical—compresses the typical sequence and urban imagery
of a rake's progress into a brief narrative, even as it sets out
Fielding's distinctive, sometimes obsessive opposition of
country and city.[4] The plot, of course, is of a feather sinking.
To a rapt Parson Adams and Joseph, Mr. Wilson relates how
at the age of seventeen he broke his late father's will, pocketed
his inheritance, and hurried into London, where precisely
like Hogarth's Tom Rakewell he made his first step the pur-
chase of a fine gentleman's clothing. This concern with fashionable costume (I "took my great stick, and walked out in
my green frock, with my hair in papers [*a groan from
Adams*])," harmless enough as a London phenomenon,
nonetheless glides quickly into a concern with "fashionable
phrases"; and the vanity of periwig and frock swells into the
vanity of false reputation for intrigues. Wilson confesses that
he has sometimes counterfeited billets-doux to himself or in
the encouraging atmosphere of a tavern displayed a paper,
"perhaps a tailor's bill, and kissed it, crying out at the same
time, 'By Gad, I was once fond of her.' " His oath, which
Adams instantly reproves, points only too well to the future.
Caught in a lie and refusing to duel, Wilson spirals eastward
and downward across London, from Westminster to Covent
Garden and the Temple (reversing the direction of the
Dunces), fitfully blazing with venereal disease until he lands
at last in debtor's prison, an extinguished spark, to await a
providential rescue.

By-now-familiar motifs like clothing and playhouses appear
in his story as agents of corruption; so too does the Londoner's
blindness to true and false language (we notice that as his
fortune evaporates his language deteriorates into "nothing
but noise: singing, hollowing, wrangling, drinking, toasting,
sp——wing, smoking were the chief ingredients of our entertainment"). Indeed, reduced to paupery, like so many desperate
men before him he resolves for a time to live by writing—hack
plays, poems, translations, even mere scrivening. But Fielding

arranges events so that stress falls chiefly upon the promiscuous sexuality of London and only secondarily upon its abuse of language. Town women, whether of quality or prostitutes, are the candles toward which Wilson flies. Burned, he reviles them like a modern-day Juvenal, his anger transforming them into urban artifacts with bodies like "painted palaces, inhabited by Disease and Death." The artful lies of a coquette (one of several city words he must explain to Adams) are typical of the possibilities London offers for false relationships, theatrically artificial passions. Yet bad as they are, such perversions of language fade before the perversions of London sexuality. Flirtations and intrigues lead Wilson to far more reprehensible debauchings of innocent girls—one of whom descends to the streets and ends her miserable life in Newgate—and to the cuckolding of a worthy citizen, whose wife at length divorces him; others like his fellow Templars and the wife-stealing member of his "Rule-of-Right" club behave no better. This wild, abandoned sexuality so frequently associated with London is, of course, one way of expressing the city's chaotic effect upon human nature. The loss of self-control that London permits—encourages—can be seen too in its drunkenness, its gambling, even its politics and sports, but in Wilson's story Fielding seems to attack the city not so much for these causes as for the disastrous impact it has upon domesticity. Wilson and the others leave behind them too plain a trail of shattered families, the wreckage of precisely that symbol of social order which ideally a great city, a civilizing mother, ought to protect.

It is a criticism implicit in other moralizing attacks upon London vice in the early eighteenth century—even Moll Flanders preaches to a client about the harm he risks to his family—though whether because of his own domestic happiness with Charlotte Craddock, or his experiences as Bow Street magistrate, or simply because of that ironic clarity we like to call Augustan, Fielding complicates the attack by placing in opposition to the diseased ladies of the town another kind of woman altogether. Mr. Wilson is rescued from prison by Harriet Hearty, "the handsomest creature in the

universe," who first restores him to prosperity and then retires with him to the country. This labored polarity of coquette and hearty, of London and retirement, might in lesser
hands be far too simple or even childish: these are the witches
and princesses, the psychological landscapes of fairy tales.
But they are also recurrent terms in Fielding's writing that
permit a complex and deeply felt denunciation of the poison
which, to his mind, London releases into English moral life.

In all of his fiction the great city appears as corrupt and
corrupting, the country for all its flaws as wholesome. *Tom
Jones* (1749), seven years after *Joseph Andrews,* abandons
the general plot of a rake's progress but expands the scale of
London wickedness. The opposition of rural and urban is less
forced—the Gypsy caravan, for example, forms a contrast to
the town masquerade more subtle than any effect in the near-
farce of *Joseph Andrews*—and Tom's long sojourn in London
seems even a necessary stage in his education: a purgatorial
episode where he is to learn directly of the consequences of
excess and to distinguish between the innocent deceits of a
Molly Seagrim or Black George and the brittle, masked insincerity of a Lady Bellaston. The famous visit to the playhouse
serves in part to reveal Tom's growing taste for truthfulness
in art as well as life (Partridge sneers at Garrick's natural performance, preferring the king: "he speaks all his words distinctly, half as loud again as the other.—Anybody may see he
is an actor").[5] The affected and obscure language of the
town, afterward lightly mocked in Fielding's "Modern Glos-
sary," for the *Covent-Garden Journal,* is similarly penetrated
and identified as bombast.[6] But if Tom proceeds through
these urban snares with a general surefootedness, unlike his
counterpart Nightingale, nonetheless an atmosphere of ominous gesture, casual power remains to threaten him. Lady
Bellaston troubles us more deeply than Lady Booby; Lord
Fellamar represents an actual menace. The aura of Restoration comedy so often noted in the London section of the
novel shares with actual Restoration drama a basis of cruel
sensuality, of sexual duels like those between certain arach-
nid insects, gossamer and deadly. The press gang that stalks

Tom emerges for a moment from the city's underworld; otherwise Fielding seems uninterested in depicting the vast, uncertain London beyond Westminster, and we move only across fashionable stage sets, through houses, rooms, windows, while a feeling of enclosure, of indoors rather than outdoors rapidly develops. It is no surprise to follow both Tom and Sophia into literal places of confinement, she in a series of chambers, he in the Gatehouse prison near Westminster Abbey.

Nor is it a surprise to find Fielding's last major work built around entrances and exits to Newgate. "Fielding drops his high spirits whenever he writes about London," as George Sherburn observes.[7] And *Amelia* (1751) in particular adapts the devices of masquerades and prisons, the polarity of good woman (Amelia herself) and bad women (Miss Matthews, Mrs. Trent) to depressing diatribes against the city. Like all of Fielding's portraits, this London lacks concrete or visual details; it exists almost exclusively as middle-class and aristocratic talk, but its bitter adulteries, drugged seductions, and hypocritical intrigues—far more destructive than in the earlier novels—suggest a widespread unraveling of English society. (See especially *Amelia,* XI, 2). In the end an abrupt and implausible change of fortune sends Amelia and her husband, like other chosen characters in Fielding, to a secure retreat in the country. Ronald Paulson compares this movement to Juvenal's third *Satire,* in which the corruptions of Rome drive its most virtuous (and truly Roman) citizens away from the heart of the nation, bitterly cursing the city.[8] But Fielding's novels are most commonly compared to the epics they broadly mock, and in that context we may also remember how epic cities like Rome or Carthage sometimes seem to collapse from the burden of historical progress, from the simple advance of time and fate, as well as from their own iniquities.

II

Despite the personal vision that shapes such narratives and selects such images, Fielding's sober attacks upon the city be-

long to a more general trend of London malediction prominent in the literature of midcentury. These attacks are not
to be confused with the pamphlet exposés of low-life earlier
described. For just as Fielding appears uninterested in portraying the lower-class life of the city, so other midcentury
portraits also fasten in a general way upon the failings of
aristocracy and its slavish middle-class imitators. And much
of this vituperation, understandably, is generated by the indistinct but palpable mood of the country as the long Walpole
ministry comes to an end in the early 1740s and as the nation,
oddly listless in its political goals and policy, seeks ways to
excoriate a sense of failed purpose: almost as if, deprived of
its accustomed target, the anti-Walpolean anger spills aim-
lessly back and forth out of inertia.[9]

One important early complaint stands at the head of a long
and growing line of attack. Johnson's *London,*[10] an imitation
of Juvenal's third *Satire,* was published in May of 1738
(oddly, the same month and year as John Wesley's conversion
on Aldergate Street, which launched the reforming energies
of Methodism). As in the *Dunciad,* the decaying physical life
of the city represents its decaying moral life—

> And now a rabble rages, now a fire;
> Their ambush here relentless ruffians lay,
> And here the fell attorney prowls for prey;
> Here falling houses thunder on your head,
> And here a female atheist talks you dead.
>
> [14–18]

And masquerades, licentious theater, opera, foreign refugees,
and greedy stockjobbers are all named as symptoms of decline. Walpole figures largely in the satire, a judgment Johnson came to regret, as does the "Senatorian band,/Whose
Ways and Means support the sinking land" (244–45), and
against them stands the lost *beatum tempus* of Alfred and
Eliza. The most memorable lines of the poem, however, concern not the malaise of London but Johnson's own struggles
for literary recognition in the city. Nearly thirty at the time,
obscure and living on slender savings while he labored to finish

his tragedy *Irene,* he had left Oxford without a degree almost ten years earlier for lack of money, had accomplished little since, and was now beginning to write piecework for booksellers like Edmund Cave. Suddenly his own accumulated frustrations break through the constraints of imitation, and forecast the later Johnson's moral themes and moral vigor:

> Quick let us rise, the happy seats explore,
> And bear oppression's insolence no more.
> This mournful truth is ev'ry where confess'd,
> SLOW RISES WORTH, BY POVERTY DEPRESS'D:
> But here more slow, where all are slaves to gold,
> Where looks are merchandise, and smiles are sold;
> Where won by bribes, by flatteries implor'd,
> The groom retails the favours of his lord.
>
> [174–81]

Boswell rightly concentrates on this personal note in his discussion, and later readers have likewise slighted Juvenalian echoes to wonder instead if Thales represents Richard Savage or if Johnson's tone is self-reflexively ironic. More comprehensive satire of the un-Roman city can be found in the Horatian imitations Pope published in the same year, with their spacious sweep of political and social allusions and their thickets of proper names drawn from all ranks of the town. Pope strikes from another kind of frustration, of course, a disgust with fraudulent commercialism and the erosion of public standards, and the backdrop of these poems is a denser, more realistic city than Johnson's. Yet through it rings the same dismal cry of "London's voice: 'Get Mony, Mony still!/ And then let Virtue follow, if she will.' "[11]

Both poets, celebrated and obscure, are writing from the perspective of Tory satire. Much more typical of the post-Walpolean lassitude is John Brown's anguished *Estimate of the Manners and Principles of the Times* (1757), largely forgotten now but perversely popular when it first appeared, the work of a constitutionally melancholy clergyman (who later committed suicide) which berates the effeminacy of the English nation and calls urgently for moral reform. As we

might expect, Brown holds up for ridicule most London pas-
times (beginning with an attack on foppish dress) and theorizes
that commerce, necessary to a nation in its youth and fueled
by a great metropolis, ultimately spells its luxurious doom,
an idea that with variations also preoccupied Defoe. Other
writers like the anti-Jacobite James Burgh in *Britain's Remembrancer; or, The Danger Not Over* (1746) warn against
London luxury, against the depopulation of the island—a
point seized upon by American colonists—and against a
wholesale weakening of moral fiber. *"O London, London,"*
he cries like a modern Jeremiah, "how hast thou degenerated!"
The good old days have been betrayed by "LUXURY and
IRRELIGION":

> In every street of this great Metropolis [an observer] will
> see one Tavern or House of Entertainment within Call of
> another; whereas it is known, that only in the Days of the
> Fathers of People now alive, strong Liquors were sold no
> where but at the Shops of Apothecaries. In the Dress of
> the Inhabitants he will see Journeymen and Chamber-
> maids got beyond the Pitch of the Quality of the last
> Age.[12]

It is in this same period that Henry Fielding published an
Enquiry into the Causes of the Late Increase of Robbers
(1751), concluding that London luxury was a major cause of
rising crime; a "perversion" of relaxation carried to scanda-
lous excess,

> especially in and near the Metropolis, where the Places
> of Pleasure are almost become numberless: for besides
> those great Scenes of Rendezvous, where the Nobleman
> and his Taylor, the Lady of Quality and her Tirewoman,
> meet together and form one common Assembly, what
> an immense Variety of Places have this Town and its
> Neighbourhood set apart for the Amusement of the lowest
> Order of the People; and where the Master of the House,
> or Wells, or Garden, may be said to angle only in the
> Kennels, where baiting with the vilest Materials, he catches
> only the thoughtless and tastless Rabble.[13]

Two years later he was called to organize a more efficient London constabulary after citizens had protested to authorities the terrifying rise of violent crime in the streets. His half-brother Sir John Fielding, the "Blind Beak," assumed the work after his death and in 1758, reporting on the successful reduction of crime, nonetheless continued the cry against the city's wanton idleness. In the country, he argued, laborers are content with regular holidays and innocent sports.

> But in this Town, Diversions calculated to slacken the Industry of the useful Hands are innumerable . . . Bull-baitings, Bear-baitings, Cock-matches, and such Races as are contrary to Law, are in the Number of out-door Diversions that call for Redress. . . . But the Amusements of the greatest Consequence are those that are carried on in the Public-Houses in Town; such as Cards, Dice, Draughts, Shuffle-boards, Missisippi [sic] Tables, Billiards, and cover'd Skittle-Grounds. These are the Thieves that rob the Journeymen and Labourers of their precious Time, their little Propserity, and their less Morals.[14]

These attacks reach something like a crescendo in a series of letters from London written by Matt Bramble in Smollett's *Humphrey Clinker* (1771). There a reluctant nod of approval for the improved lighting and pavement of Westminster and the City is quickly followed by an anatomy of annoyances. "The capital is become an overgrown monster," Bramble declares, "which, like a dropsical head, will in time leave the body and extremities without nourishment and support."[15] Worse still, "the tide of luxury has swept all the inhabitants from the open country" and deposited them like silt in London, where they lounge in fine clothes, insult their betters, and take finally to crime, secure in the "immense wilderness of the city" in which no police or watch can apprehend them. Bramble objects to the democratic jumble of the city—"there is no distinction or subordination left"—and his language focuses upon the monstrosity of a society where nothing can be clarified or fixed into plan; the opulent clothing of the masses, masquerades, the cascade of sights in the streets or the amusement parks of Vauxhall and Ranelagh, the deceptiveness of every assembly all offend him by the violence they do to civic order. Naturally enough, he phrases his disgust in images of disease, condemning the putrefactive air of London, the "maukish contents of an open aquaduct" which he must drink, the poisonous bleaching of London bread for the sake of fashion; nothing is regulated, nothing is natural in the city and, wistfully quoting Horace, he longs for the unpolluted country. Such images of physical corruption reach a logical climax in images of mental sickness:

> The hodcarrier, the low mechanic, the tapster, the publican, the shopkeeper, the pettifogger, the citizen, and courtier, *all tread upon the kibes of one another:* actuated by the demons of profligacy and licentiousness, they are seen every where rambling, riding, rolling, rushing, justling, mixing, bouncing, cracking, and crashing in one vile ferment of stupidity and corruption—All is tumult and hurry; one would imagine they were impelled by some disorder of the brain, that will not suffer them to be at rest.

Bramble speaks in character, of course. Other voices in the novel find other ways to respond to the assault of the city, more admiring and more tolerant. But Bramble is sounding a theme heard frequently in the mid and later eighteenth century: the conviction that the sheer complexity of urban life, its artificial and insatiable demands upon the spirit, is responsible for a uniquely modern derangement. To ride in carriages or sedan chairs instead of walking, to rise at noon and to retire at midnight, to breathe congested air and tremble at the constant sound of traffic, to pass anonymously through crowds of strangers, fearful of their violence but indifferent to their misery—such habits of life, which we may have thought a twentieth-century affliction, contribute to an early urban anxiety. A gigantic Bedlam increasingly becomes an image for the city. The devils once thought to inhabit the forests are transplanted into its streets and slums, leaving the natural world a more innocent and more inviting place than ever before in European history. And for eighteenth-century

England, a time of growing historical sensibility, one additional cause for nervousness about the size and wickedness of London now appears. Again and again at midcentury the pattern of the Roman Empire is evoked in comparison with English national decay, the tumultuous folly of London seen as a precursor of destruction. In the largest sense, all of our texts from the *Dunciad* on have measured London against the omnipresent backdrop of Roman history: Fielding's and Smollett's satires implicitly, Johnson's, Brown's, and the others' explicitly. (Burgh goes further and lists the Assyrian, Babylonian, and Persian empires as well.) The body-state analogy so frequently applied to classical history is found to apply equally well to the English nation, with its diseased and overgrown capital. The extraordinary wealth of London— in reality herald of a rising, not collapsing empire—suggests the image of Rome fatted and fallen away from a simpler heritage and besieged by the barbarians.[16] Gibbon, whose motives can never be pried free from his irony, does not openly gauge England's future by Rome's past in *The Decline and Fall of the Roman Empire* (1776). But in chapter 31 he sets out with unmistakable design the similarities between the two states, dwelling on the effeminacy of the upper classes, especially their concern with dress and food and amusement, and recoiling like the fastidious Bramble himself from their opposites: the "swarm of dirty and ragged plebians, without shoes and without a mantle; who loitered away whole days in the street or Forum to hear news and to hold disputes; who dissipated in extravagant gaming the miserable pittance of their wives and children; and spent the hours of the night in obscure taverns and brothels in the indulgence of gross and vulgar sensuality."[17] Not alone did the London rake plunge downward from pleasure to pleasure toward spectacular, utter ruin.

III

"After unpacking my trunk," Boswell writes in his rooms in Piccadilly late in the spring of 1768, "I sallied forth like a roaring Lion after girls, blending philosophy and raking."[18]

Boswell's London follies are not to be confused with national or historic moods; they are purely and merely personal explosions of temperament, detonated by the contact of Londonian ether with his own inflammable personality. The most famous account of them is the great *London Journal* of 1762–63, his first lengthy attempt at a record of his own experience, which was mailed off in weekly batches to his friend John Johnston of Grange and published at last almost two centuries later in 1950. We read Boswell's journal for the drama of his meeting with Samuel Johnson late in his stay, sensing the operations of fate as it forms the biographer-to-be, and for the related drama of his conflicts with his distant father over the course of his future; but chiefly we read the *London Journal* for the extraordinary picture it supplies of every side of the great city, unique in eighteenth-century literature, and for the extraordinary relationship Boswell establishes between himself and its whole vast range of life. At all points in his career, from Scotland, Corsica, the Continent, Boswell swivels like the needle of a compass to point himself toward London. It is a place that releases and satisfies needs which otherwise circle roughly and painfully within him, though it is in no sense a place where, like Tom Jones or Mr. Wilson, he learns to control and reform those needs. "I never knew any one who had such a *gust* for London as you have," Johnson declares in wonder (B*LJ*, III, 176–77).[19]

At the most superficial level it is London's variety that thrills Boswell so remarkably. He compares it to a museum, a garden, to endless musical combinations. With friends he resolves to walk its length in a day, beginning at Hyde Park Corner in the morning, and to end the night by recrossing to Covent Garden theater; and he marvels, "the variety that we met with as we went along is amazing. As the Spectator observes, one end of London is like a different country from the other in look and manners" (*Jour.*, 153).[20] On another day, "We then walked to the Exchange, and sauntered into Guildhall. I was in good London humour and comfortable enough. We dined at Dolly's Beefsteak-house; then went to Saint Paul's Church and heard the choir chanting. In short, this was a day of great variety. We next walked into the Temple" (*Jour.*, 222). The names of London landmarks ripple through his narrative like notes in a carillon. He visits every place we might expect—St. Paul's, from whose cupola he likes to view the whole extent of the city, Covent Garden, St. James's Park, Parliament, Ranelagh and Vauxhall, the Tower, Newgate prison—and searches out surprising crannies such as Mrs. Salmon's waxwork gallery, the rooms of the Sublime Society of Beefsteaks above the Bedford Coffee House, even the Bow Churchyard publisher of children's stories he once enjoyed. When at a later date Johnson speaks of the strange modes of life to be observed in London and earnestly recommends that he *"explore Wapping,"* Boswell dutifully sets out for that distant country (though he finds it a little disappointing) (B*LJ*, IV, 201). The streets, crowds, sights of the city intoxicate him; they inspire him, he claims, with a vivacity he lacks elsewhere; they serve, to take up an inevitable image, as a gigantic, inexhaustible theater into which he skips, ready to perform or to observe entirely as he likes.

By itself, however, Boswell's love of London spectacle could hardly have propelled the *Journal* onto the best-seller lists of 1950; raking, not philosophy, has naturally extended its interest beyond scholarly chambers. At the same time, though they enliven the book immeasurably, his notorious sexual escapades offer evidence, sometimes pathetic rather than amusing, of deeper needs that the city answered. Much of his debauchery, of course, results from simple youthful wildness, the high spirits of a man twenty-two years old, far from a disapproving parent, with £200 as annual allowance, and "surrounded with numbers of free-hearted ladies of all kinds: from the splendid Madam at fifty guineas a night, down to the civil nymph with white-thread stockings who tramps along the Strand and will resign her engaging person to your honour for a pint of wine and a shilling" (*Jour.*, 83–84). But Boswell's transactions with London prostitutes also allow us to glimpse for a moment the coarse, disheartening world that always lies just beyond the boundaries of urban glamour. "As I was coming home this night," he records after an incongruous discussion of monarchy and republicanism,

> I felt carnal inclinations raging through my frame. I determined to gratify them. I went to St. James's Park, and, like Sir John Brute, picked up a whore. For the first time did I engage in armour, which I found but a dull satisfaction. She who submitted to my lusty embraces was a young Shropshire girl, only seventeen, very well-looked, her name Elizabeth Parker. Poor being, she has a sad time of it! [*Jour.*, 227]

Not long after he saunters into the park again:

> and took the first whore I met, whom I without many words copulated with free from danger, being safely sheathed. She was ugly and lean and her breath smelt of spirits. I never asked her name. When it was done, she slunk off. I had a low opinion of this gross practice and resolved to do it no more. [*Jour.*, 231]

At other times his appetite carries him on patrol into Covent Garden, with its two theaters and several taverns long the undisputed center of London entertainment. "As the Exchange is the heart of LONDON," Steele had cheerfully declared, speaking of the usual divisions of the city; "the *great Hall,* and all under the contiguous roofs, the heart of WESTMINSTER; so is *Covent-Garden* the heart of THE TOWN."[21] It had, however, grown less reputable with the years, and in 1730 the local tradesmen had gone so far as to ask the government for relief from its lawlessness. ("The pick-pockets," Shenstone writes in a letter of 1743, "formerly content with mere filching, make no scruple to knock people down with bludgeons in Fleet-street and the Strand, and that at no later hour than eight o'clock at night: but in the Piazzas, Covent-garden, they come in large bodies, armed with couteaus, and attack whole parties"—BLJ, I, 163, n.2). The Hummums bathhouse on the southeast side of the Piazza doubled as a popular brothel, and Tom King's Coffee-house in front of St. Paul's church (pictured in its usual rowdy confusion in

Hogarth's "Morning") attracted an unfastidious and shop-worn set of prostitutes; the neighborhood around housed more expensive women, who were often described in chapbooks such as the *List of the Sporting Ladies* (London, c. 1770) and *Harris' List of Covent-garden Ladies* (London, c. 1788).[22]

Although Boswell plunges unhesitatingly into these scenes of sexual riot, his participation is not always merely physical. There are moments like those in St. James's Park when he simply falls to whoring, but on other occasions his behavior includes an element of fantasy, of acting out that is both Boswellian and characteristically urban. Every reader notices how often Boswell instructs himself to "be" like one or another hero, like Addison or Digges or like his father; and these private injunctions can be easily enough explained by Boswell's innate plasticity, his lifelong love of mimicry—in which he reminds us of his Protean contemporary, Casanova—and by his repeated attempts to bring into focus all the warring factors of his own character. But Boswell's sexual adventures seem also connected with his habitual impersonations. He acts like Addison in order to gain dignity, reserve, stability—in short, to be like his father. He acts like Macheath or Digges (who played the part of Macheath in Edinburgh), however, to assert himself aggressively and yet obliquely, to express his sense of isolation and insecurity in the great city, and to give to his sexual energies a role in his identity from which they were normally excluded by polite convention. Much of this is harmless and even winning. When he walks up and down Fleet Street on the morning after he has first enjoyed Louisa, he thinks on London, "the seat of Parliament and the seat of pleasure," and imagines himself "one of the wits in King Charles the Second's time" (*Jour.,* 140). He calls upon a young prostitute, Miss Watts, and poses as a rough Highlander named Macdonald. But frustrated by an interruption, he steals from her apartment into Covent Garden and accosts two women, whom he leads into a private room of the Shakespeare's Head Tavern. There "I toyed with them and drank about and sung *Youth's the Season* and thought myself Captain Macheath; and then I solaced my existence with them, one after the other, according to their seniority" (*Jour.*, 264).

No student of Boswell's life would claim that London is the sole stage for such theatrical debauchery, yet London stimulates him to extraordinary exhibitions. During one famous evening in particular he seems to dangle the key to his own personality and to suggest how complete is the conjunction of sexuality, city, and impersonation. On June 4, 1763, the king's birthnight, Boswell resolves to dress as a blackguard (a term associated primarily with London, but also the reverse of Royal Guard) and to roam the holiday streets in search of the usual adventure. In the park he "picked up a low brimstone, called myself a barber and agreed with her for sixpence. . . ." In the Strand he bargains with another "profligate wretch," but encountering resistance he switches identities again and roars to the interested mob of whores and soldiers, "Brother soldiers, should not a half-pay officer r-g-r for sixpence?" Thwarted and abusing her, as he says, in blackguard style, he retreats to Whitehall and yet another girl, to whom he calls himself a highwayman and then returns home "gratified tonight that, notwithstanding of my dress, I was always taken for a gentleman in disguise" (*Jour.*, 272–73). Boswell's delight in these low roles testifies, no doubt, to his forlornness in the city and to his frustration at being excluded from the elite Guards; his highwayman pose (he is ordinarily quite frightened of them when he travels) suggests an inversion of superego clearly related to struggles with his judicial father. Moreover, this dissolving of identity and subsequent reassurance help for a moment to rid him of the Scottishness that all along plagues him in London, where Lord Bute, a Scotsman, had recently deposed the great commoner Pitt and where Scotsmen in general were scornfully mocked and resented by the people, even sometimes assaulted or mobbed. The king's birthnight suits such evasive purposes exactly (and we can see the impulse in another instance, when Boswell dedicated a whole day to behaving like an Englishman). These are concrete causes for his attraction to disguises in London, linked with his love of the theater (and actresses) and with the volatility of his own nature; they seem unrelated to the Weltschmerz of the nineteenth century or to later existential posturing, urban or otherwise. Yet when we recall Moll Flanders's similar habits of disguise and impersonation in London, a difference is felt immediately. Moll's acting has the single-minded goal of profit, nothing more; she takes advantage of the unconnectedness of the city, without allowing it to touch her central, inner self. Though her adventures tease us with their suggestions of alienation and modernity, she remains primarily a descendant of the surviving, adapting heroes of epic and voyage like Odysseus. But Boswell's disguises, when all other explanations are sifted and sorted, retain their tie with his self-conscious emotional response to the city: they help to account for our impression that his London is a stage for the discovery and display of personality, and they spur us to speculate that in certain ways he thereby represents a new and modern urban man.

Bertrand Bronson, proceeding on the reasonable assumption that what spins so constantly as Boswell must have a center, postulates two parts to his personality: the actor who turns and the observer who records; and the observer appears to Bronson the deeper, the more vital half, the center.[23] (In this Boswell reminds us of that other giant egoist of the eighteenth century, Jean Jacques Rousseau, with whom he strikes up an easy, almost predictable rapport.) London, moreover, mobilizes constantly both sides of this disjunctive self. Like Rousseau, Boswell complains of his awkwardness in company, his buffoonery and mistakes, which conceal noble qualities and mislead his public. He notes with relief that "The freedom from remark and petty censure, with which life may be passed [in London], is a circumstance which a man who knows the teazing restraint of a narrow circle must relish highly." In a city, he reflects, a man is not always obliged to be upon his best behavior. "There and there alone, a man's own house is truly his castle." And he quotes with warm approval the observation of a friend who finds the chief advantage of London "that a man is always *so near his burrow*" (B*LJ,* III, 378–79).

The divided egoist, in short, requires a proscenium and a curtain, a rhythm of presentation and withdrawal, of prominence and seclusion. But the need for attention is always pressing clamorously forward. Hence Boswell makes London an arena in which to strive for fame, notice of any kind. At a fashionable rout he is pleased to "observe people looking at me with envy, as a man of some distinction and a favourite of my Lady's. Bravo! thought I. I am sure I deserve to be a favourite. It was curious to find of how little consequence each individual was in such a crowd" (*Jour.,* 71). London authors like Goldsmith and Sheridan thrill him with ambitions of literary distinction. The oratory of Pitt kindles him to imagine a Parliamentary career. Garrick predicts, perhaps in earnest, a bright future: "What he meant by my being a great man," Boswell confesses, "I can understand. For really, to speak seriously, I think there is a blossom about me of something more distinguished than the generality of mankind" (*Jour.,* 161). (But he inwardly fears that the blossom will be nipped or blighted.)

The division of Boswell's personality into observing and performing halves may be unfair to the latter, however. The image, after all, is theatrical, and no actor is content to play a single role. Boswell's London performances, though often compulsive and automatic, are also frequently undertaken in a spirit of sheer delight with his own facility, in the special mood of rich expansiveness that London inspires. Nothing so interests him as to contemplate his own unbounded plenitude:

> What a singular being do I find myself! Let this my journal show what variety my mind is capable of. But am I not well received everywhere? Am I not particularly taken notice of by men of the most distinguished genius? And why? I have neither profound knowledge, strong judgment, nor constant gaiety. But I have a noble soul which still shines forth, a certain degree of knowledge, a multiplicity of ideas of all kinds. . . . I can tune myself to the tone of any bearable man I am with that he is as much at freedom as with another self.[24]

When we recall that it is precisely the variety of London that so attracts and pleases him, Boswell's delight takes on additional significance. Does not London's multiplicity match his own? At some intuitive level does he not establish an identification between city and self? At every point the fact of *change* has characterized eighteenth-century London—its uncontrollable physical growth in Defoe, its fluidity of crowds and sights, its flow of fashion and language and distraction. And these are the terms that also describe Boswell's sense of his own personality: fragmented, theatrical, astonishingly mixed, and containing backways of depravity and coarseness as well as features of sublimity, a constant traffic of emotion that extends across the limits of his consciousness. These are likewise terms that describe the more general literary sensibility emerging in the later eighteenth century. Rousseau has imagined, called for a new man, whose strong inner core of identity will nourish an endlessly changing exterior self. Other writers like Sterne, Chatterton, Ossian, Smart, and Blake—those whom Northrop Frye assigns to the "age of sensibility"—share at least this restlessness of personality.[25] Their fascination with the process of self resembles Boswell's. And if they do not always join him before the mirror of the city, that may be in part because Boswell's consuming egoism simply outdistances theirs and leaps forward toward a later generation of urban sensibility, that delimited by Baudelaire and Dickens.

In the case of Boswell, whatever the validity of these speculations, we can say with confidence that London partakes of his every mood, exultant or depressed, and faithfully reflects it. He casts himself into it, pleased always to meet a response equal to his own conceptions. No doubt some share of this dynamic, reciprocal relationship can be explained by Boswell's remarkable attachment simply to place. When he sets out from Edinburgh, for example, in November 1762 to begin the long journey to London, he orders the driver of his chaise to halt at the edge of the town while he bows a farewell to its ancient buildings; and he does not neglect to bow "thrice to Arthur Seat, that lofty romantic mountain on which I have so often strayed in the days of my youth, indulged meditation and felt the raptures of a soul filled with ideas of the magnificence of GOD and his creation" (*Jour.*, 41–42). The editor of the journal compares in a note Boswell's love of place with the romanticism of Sir Walter Scott. On the basis of this and dozens of other such scenes, we may be tempted to extend the comparison to a second romantic, Wordsworth, whose devotion to place, like Boswell's, usually reveals a profound identification between self and setting. And Wordsworth's landscapes gradually take shape as the vision of a sublime Other, a tutoring, scolding, eternal being distinct from the poet and yet finally understood to belong to his own limitless personality. It is hard not to remember that, although he had no inkling in 1762 when he reboarded his chaise for London, Boswell was hurrying toward a meeting with his own sublime other. Even then Samuel Johnson may have been rolling and puffing down the Strand toward Tom Davies's bookshop in Russell Street, a tutoring, scolding being inseparable from the great city that sustained him.

IV

Johnson in London conjures up one of the most captivating pageants of literary mythology. Everyone who reads treasures the folk image of the Great Cham navigating the full tide of human existence at Charing Cross, pronouncing London synonymous with life, bounding at three in the morning from his chambers in the Temple to greet Beauclerk and Langton: "What, is it you, you dogs! I'll have a frisk with you," and sallying with them to Covent Garden, a tavern, Billingsgate (B*LJ*, I, 250). Our lasting impression from Boswell's *Life* and journals is of Johnson's extraordinary love of London. When we think of the life captured (but not stilled) in those pages, we are apt to recall Johnson at the Mitre, at Bolt Court, over a bowl of punch; we are apt to identify him, as Boswell certainly did, with the immense variety of his city and with its abundant, exuberant energy; we are apt to think of him as a force, blowing through London's vast extent as naturally, as constantly as wind and traffic. It is a fact that the student of his life likely takes for granted, but it is a fact worth pausing over; for Johnson's love of London distinguishes him from almost all of the major writers we have been considering. Defoe, Pope, Swift, Fielding are entangled in London, their fates are tied to it; but without exception they picture an apocalyptic city, doomed by its own energy and carrying them downward with it. Wordsworth and Blake will similarly resist its bright, enervating magnetism. Only Gay among our writers expresses in *Trivia* something like Johnson's satisfaction with the city, and even then a reader is tempted to conflate the dim irony of that poem and the brightly comic urban satire of *The Beggar's Opera.* Johnson's London, however, is not an apocalyptic city, or a city gone wild with growth, or a blight upon England's green and pleasant hills. He denies that luxury is corrupting London's former virtue, that it resembles a head too great for its body, that it has fallen from the imagined perfection of Jerusalem and Rome, that such abstract categories apply at all to our authentic experience of things. In contrast with the others, he never invokes an ideal city against which to measure what he sees: as always, his instinct is for the actual.

If not Babylon or Rome, therefore, neither is Johnson's London the Happy Valley. "I wandered about [Lichfield] for five days," he writes Joseph Baretti wearily in 1762, "and took the first convenient opportunity of returning to a place where, if there is not much happiness, there is at least such a diversity of good and evil, that slight vexations do not fix upon the heart."[26] A sense of that evil rolls powerfully through the formality of *London,* as we have seen, but we must wait until another work, written almost six years later, for the terms and themes to emerge that make his city not merely a stage for literary pageantry, but also a tribunal for the moral life.

Johnson wrote the *Life of Richard Savage* (1744) in the early winter of 1743, when he was thirty-four. For the three previous years he had followed the steady though not lucrative employment of writing up Parliamentary Debates for the *Gentleman's Magazine;* translations, prefaces, biographies,

and other bits of journalism had further established him in
Grub Street; Tetty Johnson had joined him in London, and a
faint but discernible respectability now clung to his life. The
memory of Savage, however, dated from the period not much
earlier when Johnson had grappled with that category of
poverty he later defined as "want of necessaries" and together
with Savage had roamed the dangerous, unfriendly city, without prospects, but not without spirit.[27] "He told Sir Joshua
Reynolds, that one night in particular, when Savage and he
walked round St. James's-square for want of a lodging, they
were not at all depressed by their situation; but in high spirits
and brimful of patriotism, traversed the square for several
hours, inveighed against the minister, and 'resolved they
would *stand by their country*' "(B*LJ,* I, 164). But to labor at
hackwork was not Johnson's ambition. To toss in strained
domesticity with an aging wife quieted little of his restlessness. Beneath the surface the contemplation of Savage's
bizarre, disastrous career seemed to provoke a scrutiny of
his own. In many respects the *Life of Savage* became the
story of his own life.[28]

Savage, it is true, that luxuriantly reckless man, cruised
down the broad avenues of dissipation *suo motu,* flying both
from pleasure to pleasure and from hope to hope without the
least hindrance of scruples or self-control. (He once thought
of writing a poem on the subject of the rake's progress, to be
called *The Progress of a Free-Thinker,* based in large part
upon his own experience.) Every scrap of money or advantage he obtained he squandered, every friend discarded; he
touched several times the extremes of destitution and fortune, notoriety and obscurity, and died penniless at last in
a grim provincial jail. Less even than Boswell was he capable
of systematic conduct. This is not at first glance a portrait of
Johnson, who has come to stand in many minds as an allegorical figure for sturdiness, conservatism, probity. But from
the first, readers have noted the preternatural intensity of the
narrative and the prominence of the narrator's voice. As
Savage comes to exasperate us by his hotheaded antics, Johnson's compassionate engagement with such a pathology in-

creasingly fascinates; and slowly, in retrospect we realize that however often his compassion pushes outward to inclusive moral judgments ("By Arts like these, Arts which every Man practises in some Degree . . ." *Life of Savage,* p. 73), it also circles back continually to his own bedeviled preoccupations. We read passages like this with a start of recognition: "he went in with them to a neighbouring Coffee-house, and sat drinking till it was late, it being in no Time of Mr. *Savage*'s Life any Part of his Character to be the first of the Company that desire to separate" (31). "He mingled in cursory Conversation with the same Steadiness of Attention as others apply to a Lecture" (136). "He excelled in the arts of Conversation, and therefore willingly practised them: He had seldom any Home, or even a Lodging in which he could be private, and therefore was driven into public Houses for the common Conveniences of Life" (104). "His Mind was in an uncommon Degree vigorous and active. His Judgment was accurate, his Apprehension quick, and his Memory so tenacious, that he was frequently observed to know what he had learned from others in a short Time better than those by whom he was informed" (136). Other parallels are often noted: the pride of the two men in the midst of distress (hence Savage scorns the unceremonious gift of clothing from a well-wisher, just as Johnson at Oxford had ignored the new shoes left at his door by a friend); their theatrical ambitions for poetical tragedies; their scorn for prudence and for condescension. Johnson's plainly ambiguous feelings toward his mother—feelings extended and complicated by his marriage—have likewise been seen reflected in the melodramatic story of Savage's heartless mother, which Johnson accepted uncritically, and the intervention of improbably good woman like Mrs. Oldfield and the queen.[29]

The comparison reaches to one further parallel: both Savage and Johnson are almost impossible to imagine apart from London. London is their library, they immerse themselves in it instinctively, range through it tirelessly, delight in knowing its remotest, most unexpected recesses. In the *Life of Savage,* our impression of this voracious urbanity is built up unobtrusively, not by means of concrete descriptions or of open declarations, but rather by an accumulation of details, characters, and places: coffeehouses, printers' offices, courtrooms and prisons, the rooms of petty taverns and the levees of the great; blustering judges, conniving whores, patient comrades—they pass by naturally, largely unnoticed by us, particles of life suspended in the atmosphere of the story. Yet London serves as more than backdrop. The random, accidental quality of urban life suits a strong disorderly, frankly rebellious element in their personalities. Savage slips erratically across the whole face of London, searching out new regions as progressively his credit or his friendships are exhausted. (Moll Flanders and Mr. Wilson criss-cross the city in the same tempo of establishment and flight.) Johnson can sketch this randomness quickly, neutrally:

> During a considerable Part of the Time, in which he was employed upon this Performance, he was without Lodging, and often without Meat; nor had he any other Conveniences for Study than the Fields or the Streets allowed him, there he used to walk and form his Speeches, and afterwards step into a Shop, beg for a few Moments the Use of the Pen and Ink, and write down what he had composed upon Paper which he had picked up by Accident. [*Life of Savage,* 21]

At other times he enlarges, to reveal both outrage and intense identification:

> In this Manner were passed those Days and those Nights, which Nature had enabled him to have employed in elevated Speculations, useful Studies, or pleasing Conversation. On a Bulk, in a Cellar, or in a Glass-house among Thieves and Beggars, was to be found the Author of the *Wanderer,* the Man of exalted Sentiments, extensive Views and curious Observations, the man whose Remarks on Life might have assisted the Statesman, whose Ideas of Virtue might have enlightened the Moralist, whose Eloquence might have influenced Senates, and whose Delicacy might have polished Courts. [97]

Arthur Murphy long ago speculated that Johnson named his first series of periodical essays the *Rambler* in tribute to Savage's best poem, *The Wanderer;* we may add that the melancholy, uprooted figure suggested by their titles must also have satisfied an urge for self-description (*JM*, I, 391).[30] The city nurtured them. It stocked their minds with extraordinary examples of motive and behavior that animate their writings. It permitted a freedom to be found nowhere else—not in Bristol, not in Lichfield—which eased the conflicting demands of their own eccentricities. Yet London, like a bad mother, also ignored them. For long stretches of time they rambled or wandered unnoticed, uncomforted in privation. However loudly St. James's Park rang with their cheers, discouragement still cankered their hopes and harried them to fits of sloth or frightening explosions of temper: "SLOW RISES WORTH, BY POVERTY DEPRESS'D." Even so,

> The great Hardships of Poverty were to *Savage* not the Want of Lodging or of Food, but the Neglect and Contempt which it drew upon him. He complained that as his Affairs grew desperate he found his Reputation for Capacity visibly decline, that his Opinion in Questions of Criticism was no longer regarded, when his Coat was out of Fashion. [*Life of Savage*, 101]

One of the buried themes of the *Life of Savage*—a theme increasingly characteristic of eighteenth-century literature—is that of personal identity. Who is Savage? the disinherited son of a countess? or the foundling of talent who has fashioned a better fate for himself in his imagination? In London either is possible. There Savage is free to rise and fall through its circles in any of a dozen roles, a rakehell, a poet, a former inmate of Newgate prison, according to his ambition and his luck. His instability of image inevitably suggests comparison with Moll Flanders and her disguises and with Boswell. But unlike Moll, Savage has no interest in secrecy. Certain himself of his own importance, yet without friends and money to confirm it, more nearly like Boswell he faces the task of calling attention to his neglected value, of somehow imposing his conviction upon others. Denied by his mother, as Johnson observes in a famous sentence, he "was therefore obliged to seek some other Means of Support, and having no Profession, became, by Necessity, an Author" (12). Behind Johnson's irony, addressed we suspect as much to himself as to Savage, lies an unsentimental recognition that authorship is the best means remaining for Savage both literally and figuratively to make a name for himself.

These issues can be taken up in a modern idiom of identity, role, publicity—they can be seen as one possible response to the challenge of urban anonymity first noticed in Defoe—but in the *Life of Savage* and in the periodical essays of the early 1750s Johnson states them in entirely classical terms, as the love of fame. Indeed, in these years he deepens and extends the meaning of this characteristically urban folly, until it can almost be said that the pursuit of reputation replaces the rake's progress as an archetypal London fable. Yet as always in Johnson's thought, a single category or issue opens irresistibly into the still larger context of the moral uses of imagination. For the love of fame, the ambition that drives so many "candidates for renown" into the city, is only one of numberless tactics by which our imaginations habitually overturn our sense of reality.[31] "He that compares what he has done with what he has left undone," Johnson writes in *Idler* 88,

> will feel the effect which must always follow the comparison of imagination with reality; he will look with contempt on his own unimportance, and wonder to what purpose he came into the world; he will repine that he shall leave behind him no evidence of his having been, that he has added nothing to the system of life, but has glided from youth to age among the crowd, without any effort for distinction.

Stirred thus by self-importance and "a desire of filling the minds of others with admiration," we may press outward from indolence and complacency to acts of virtue or piety that merit celebration: for "Praise is so pleasing to the mind of man," Johnson says in another essay, "that it is the original motive of almost all our actions" (*Rambler* 193). From an impartial and logical perspective it will plainly appear that "the love of fame is to be regulated, rather than extinguished" (*Rambler* 49). But for the great bulk of mankind, not always logical or virtuous, the love of fame too often results in a vain assertion of self; we prefer a pleasurable fantasy to a struggle for virtue. "There is, perhaps, no man," Johnson writes in *Rambler* 155, ". . . who does not intend some time to review his conduct, and to regulate the remainder of his life by the laws of virtue." But new temptations "attack him, new invitations are offered by pleasure and interest, and the hour of reformation is always delayed; . . . and the change of manners, though sincerely intended and rationally planned, is referred to the time when some craving passion shall be fully gratified, or some powerful allurement cease its importunity."

Johnson turns naturally in discussions of the vanity of fame to the example of authors, in part because no career more importunately depends upon applause, in part no doubt because Johnson always writes out of a personal knowledge of the moral challenge he describes. ("His soul was not different from that of another person," writes Mrs. Thrale, "but . . . greater" [*JM*, I, 313]). *Rambler* 2 begins with a consideration of our concern as imaginative beings with the eventual rewards of our labor—"The natural flights of the human mind are not from pleasure to pleasure, but from hope to hope"— and proceeds to daydreams and the "disease" of authors:

> A man of lively fancy no sooner finds a hint moving in his mind, than he makes momentaneous excursions to the press, and to the world, and, with a little encouragement from flattery, pushes forward into future ages, and prognosticates the honours to be paid him, when envy is extinct, and faction forgotten.

For the reasonableness of this ambition, "every catalogue of a library will furnish sufficient" evidence: a tomb "crouded with names of men, who, though now forgotten, were once no less enterprising or confident" than ourselves, "equally pleased with their own productions, equally caressed by their patrons, and flattered by their friends." But the indulgence of literary hopes in futurity is less threatening to our virtue (and our dignity) than one great present consequence of the love of fame. "No sooner can any man emerge from the crowd," Johnson says in *Rambler* 144, expanding on the theme obliquely introduced by *Rambler* 2, "and fix the eyes of the publick upon him, than he stands as a mark to the arrows of lurking calumny, and receives, in the tumult of hostility, from distant and from nameless hands, wounds not always easy to be cured." Military imagery like this reappears whenever Johnson considers the envy excited by the love of fame, because in his view no other moral flaw so savagely disrupts our peace, so pointlessly spurs us to violate "the great law of mutual benevolence": "He that falls by the attacks of interest," claims *Rambler* 183 with brutal directness, "is torn by hungry tigers; he may discover and resist his enemies. He that perishes in the ambushes of envy, is destroyed by unknown and invisible assailants, and dies like a man suffocated by a poisonous vapour, without knowledge of his danger, or possibility of contest."

These are not bad images, however, to describe the atmosphere of London into which stream the authors, beauties, country girls, and rakes of the *Rambler,* all burning with "the fever of renown" (*The Vanity of Human Wishes,* 1. 137). Fame in Johnson's city is as uncertain as prosperity in Defoe's. Pertinax the skeptic in the course of his ill-fated removal from the university to the Temple learns to describe London as "the place where everyone catches the contagion of vanity" (*Rambler* 95). Eubulus discovers merit mocked by money (*Rambler* 26). The virtuosi of *Rambler* 177 despise each others' collections and look upon their rivals as "wretches of depraved taste and narrow notions. Their conversation was, therefore, fretful and waspish, their behavior brutal, their merriment bluntly sarcastick." A young virgin comes to London in great expectations and finds that all pleasures are subverted by competition and envy:

The heart may leap for a time under a fine gown, but the

sight of a gown yet finer puts an end to rapture. . . . There is little pleasure in conversation to her whose wit is regarded but in the second place; and who can dance with ease or spirit that sees Amaryllis led out before her? She that fancies nothing but a succession of pleasures, will find herself engaged without design in numberless competitions, and mortified without provocation with numberless afflictions. [*Idler* 80]

In such a city our rage for distinction is frequently corrected not only by the malice it generates but also by the discovery of our own insignificance—a truth Johnson everywhere insists upon profoundly and which he counts as one of the great casualties of the love of fame. The town chastens our ambitions. "No place," he tells Boswell, "cured a man's vanity or arrogance so well as London; for as no man was either great or good *per se,* but as compared with others not so good or great, he was sure to find in the metropolis many his equals, and some his superiors" (B*LJ,* II, 120). *Rambler* 146 shows us a newly published author who tours the town expecting to feast on praises. But as he hurries from place to place across London, his impatience

grows violent and tumultuous; he ranges over the town with restless curiosity, and hears in one quarter of a cricket-match, in another of a pick-pocket; is told by some of an unexpected bankruptcy, by others of a turtle feast; is sometimes provoked by importunate enquiries after the white bear, and sometimes with praises of the dancing dog; he is afterwards entreated to give his judgment upon a wager about the height of the monument; invited to see a foot race in the adjacent villages; desired to read a ludicrous advertisement; or consulted about the most effectual method of making enquiry after a favourite cat.

In the immensity of London, in short, which boils with so many jostling imaginations, so many pleasures and distractions, individual importance dwindles to a level with cricket matches and lost cats. To be sure, the writer soon persuades himself that literary merit rises slowly, and retires content to await his certain, lasting reputation. "By such arts of voluntary delusion," Johnson comments gravely in a passage reminiscent of one in the *Life of Savage,* "does every man endeavour to conceal his own unimportance from himself." And he is always proposing a melancholy imagery of urban insignificance—of crowds, streets, multitudes—as antidotes for this self-delusive passion. In *The Vanity of Human Wishes* verbs of swarming, pouring, teeming all serve to dash individual hopes relentlessly into a sea of undifferentiated humanity, where single figures rise only for a moment, like specks of foam, then sink back again and vanish. In *Rasselas,* Imlac advises the astronomer to "keep this thought always prevalent, that you are only one atom of the mass of humanity, and have neither such virtue nor vice, as that you should be singled out for supernatural favours or afflictions."[32] In *Rambler* 159, remembering perhaps the long years of indifference and obscurity he had suffered in London, the pavements, bulks, and garrets he and Savage had endured, Johnson movingly sounds the same theme, with a massive, cooling humility that compels assent:

> The truth is, that no man is much regarded by the rest of world. He that considers how little he dwells upon the condition of others, will learn how little the attention of others is attracted by himself. While we see multitudes passing before us, of whom perhaps not one appears to deserve our notice, or excites our sympathy, we should remember, that we likewise are lost in the same throng, that the eye which happens to glance upon us is turned in a moment on him that follows us, and that the utmost which we can reasonably hope or fear is to fill a vacant hour with prattle, and be forgotten.

V

One factor beyond Johnson's pleasure in its variety and novelty accounts for his attachment to London. He himself suffered all his life from a fear of solitude. His nervous mannerisms—the tics and shakings of head, the mutterings under his breath, the involuntary jerks and starts—these together with the alarming ugliness of his face no doubt urged him toward company out of a deeply felt need for reassurance and affection. "I never sought to please till past thirty years old," he tells Henry Thrale, "considering the matter as hopeless" (*JM*, I, 318). Every witness testifies to his dread of loneliness. "I am very unwilling to be left alone, Sir," he confesses to William Gerard Hamilton, "and therefore I go with my company down the first pair of stairs, in some hopes that they may, perhaps, return again" (B*LJ*, I, 490). The famous conversation clubs he founded on several occasions are considered by Sir Joshua Reynolds a partial response to this fear. "Solitude to him was horror," Reynolds remembers; "nor would he ever trust himself alone but when employed in writing or reading. He has often begged me to go home with him to prevent his being alone in the coach" (*JM*, II, 221). Joseph Wood Krutch, dwelling on Johnson's physical grotesqueness and his obsessive melancholy, states it brutally, but there is no denying the central truth of the insight:

> He was almost desperately sociable because he could never be part of any society. At every feast of wit or food he was a spectator and no matter how eagerly he tried to identify himself with the city and its multifarious life, of that too he was compelled to remain a spectator. . . . For him London was not a collection of sights. It was, first of all, simply the place where the largest number and greatest variety of men were to be found and hence the place where one was least likely to feel alone.[33]

"I am a straggling," Johnson breaks out to Boswell, "I may leave this town and go to Grand Cairo without being missed here or observed there."[34]

If his need for London is in this sense pathological, nonetheless another part of his love for the city springs from a large, healthy delight in the company it does provide him. No one can miss the vitality in his habitual praises of London conversation. "Whoever has once experienced the full flow of London talk," he tells Mrs. Thrale in a phrase that reminds us of the "full tide of human existence," "when he retires to country friendships and rural sports, must either be contented to turn baby again and play with the rattle, or he will pine away like a great fish in a little pond, and die for want of his usual food" (*JM,* I, 324). And he devotes himself to this flow of conversation, not only for the exchange of ideas or for victory in argument, but also as he often says for the simple feeling of sociability, of comfort that good-humored talk arouses. In this delight he appears to us typical of his age, whose literature excels in effects of tone and allusion rather than intensity of image or symbol. One of the pleasures of reading through such a work as Lecky's *History of England in the Eighteenth Century,* after all, is to relish his descriptions of orators celebrated in their time almost beyond anything an electronic generation can comprehend—Bolingbroke, Walpole, the elder Pitt, Whitefield, Wesley, Burke. Pope and Swift are speaking, often colloquial voices. The great innovation of Boswell's *Life,* what everyone remembers best, is the still-living conversation recorded in page after page of dialogue. An atmosphere of speech irresistibly delivered envelops Johnson's London, its clubs and taverns and debates and tête-à-têtes, and makes it to our imaginations a city of ceaseless conversation. And this atmosphere Johnson with his special needs and powers breathes hungrily. "The town is my element," he writes to Dr. Brocklesby toward the end of his life; "there are my friends, there are my books . . . and there are my amusements" (B*LJ,* IV, 358–59). He can mock the "fashionable barbarism" of town talk (*Rambler* 194) or the dialects of the various regions of the city (*Rambler* 20), but when we recall the anger that Pope and Swift turn on such corruptions, the roar with which their London collapses into gibberish, Johnson's attitude warms us by its refusal to be stampeded, its broad-minded tolerance. "It is wonderful, Sir, what is to be found in London," he observes to Boswell in a sentence we could not expect to find in the earlier Augustans: "The most literary conversation that I ever enjoyed, was at the table of Jack Ellis, a money-scrivener behind the Royal Exchange, with whom I at one period used to dine generally once a week" (B*LJ,* III, 21). "Sir Joshua told me long ago,"

he writes in the same letter to Brocklesby, "that my vocation was to publick life, and I hope still to keep my station,
till GOD shall bid me *Go in peace*." Such a vocation to public
life calms those fears of solitude that undo his peace, and at
the same time throws open to him the whole vast city, neither
collapsing nor corrupting, which he discovers with such eager
satisfaction to be his "element."

   Johnson's absorption in London inevitably suggests comparison with Dickens, who likewise roamed the city day and
night and whose knowledge of its life extended into every
corner. Dickens, indeed, paced London compulsively, gathering material for his work from its vast human reservoir and
in some mysterious way generating the energy of his genius.
His love of London *impressions* is like Ned Ward's or Gay's,
unaffected, sensual. But as he walks Dickens also seems
obsessed to draw the city into a pattern by an act of creative
will, to imagine how its thousands of separate characters,
unknown to each other, are yet secretly connected; and this
connectedness is afterward manifested in his complex plots
of coincidence, an imposition of coherence not unrelated to
the images of body we have seen already in Defoe. Johnson
too delights in London impressions and exploration, of
course; he too draws special energy from the city's sheer,
abundant presence. Yet he communicates a detachment in his
surveys of the city markedly different from Dickens's connections, an ironic willingness to analyze and to leave unconnected what is only accidental. He offers no unifying plot or
image. (The landlady's chronicle of *Rambler* 161, for example, recounts a long, amusing succession of boarders, but only
to demonstrate the truth of Juvenal's observation that a
single house contains a world of variety.) It is at another level
altogether that their deepest resemblance can be found, for
these contradictory visions in fact mark progressive stages in
what J. Hillis Miller calls the humanization of a world from
which God has disappeared.[35] In Johnson and Dickens the
symbolic force of cities, apparent from earliest times in their
tutelary goddesses, their quasidivinity, has been emptied of

religious content. Neither a creature of shadowy monstrosity as for Defoe nor a faint image of a holy type such as Rome had become for Pope and others, their London takes its forms and meanings from entirely human sources. Its citizens expect no immortality, only reputation. The goddess-mother of the city—even Pope's Dulness—dwindles into the prostitutes whom Boswell pursues and Johnson befriends, the lost Anna whom De Quincey traces through Soho, the pale heroines of *Bleak House* and *Little Dorrit.* It will remain for Blake to re-transform these human figures into myth. But Johnson in particular inhabits a resolutely unsymbolic city. He responds impulsively to its purely secular realities, out of loneliness and also out of a resilient affection, much in this way:

I have passed all my days in London, until I have formed as many and intense local attachments, as any of you mountaineers can have done with dead nature. The Lighted shops of the Strand and Fleet Street, the innumerable trades, tradesmen and customers, coaches, waggons, play-houses, all the bustle and wickedness round about Covent Garden, the very women of the Town, the Watchmen, drunken scenes, rattles,—life awake, if you awake, at all hours of the night, the impossibility of being dull in Fleet Street, the crowds, the very dirt & mud, the Sun shining upon houses and pavements, the print shops, the old book stalls, parsons cheap'ning books, coffee houses, steams of soups from kitchens, the pantomimes, London itself a pantomime and a masquerade,—all these things work themselves into my mind and feed me . . . and I often shed tears in the motley Strand from fulness of joy at so much Life.[36]

This is Charles Lamb, not Johnson, in a letter to Wordsworth; but divested of Romantic stress upon the self-conscious observer, it is closer to Johnson than to Dickens. What Lamb makes us feel in this long list is the irrepressible life of the city, a life not organized or invisibly connected, as a novelist would wish it, but uplifting us even in its jumble with a deep and tearful sense of community.

"Community" rather than connectedness describes Johnson's feeling. As much as his thought is grounded in the realities of London, the city of his moral imagination is always a more extensive and general one: what he calls in *Rambler* 24 the "concatenation of society," held together by his conviction that "men are designed for the succor and comfort of each other." *Adventurer* 67, one of Johnson's few extended discussions of London, begins in the vein made familiar by Addison's *Spectator*. Somewhat perfunctorily he admires the novelty of the metropolis, then traces the emotions of a newcomer gawking at its sights and evokes the customary beehive image for so many shops and workers. His London, like Addison's and in contrast with Defoe's, appears to be a city in which, if every man labors diligently, he prospers: bankruptcy, theft, competition are for the moment absent. But in unmistakably Johnsonian fashion he is rapidly moved to see the economic structure as adumbrating the moral one. The city provokes our imaginations endlessly, impossibly. "Every man, in surveying the shops of London, sees numberless instruments and conveniences, of which, while he did not know them, he never felt the need; and yet, when use has made them familiar, wonders how life could be supported without them. Thus it comes to pass, that our desires always increase with our possessions; the knowledge that something remains yet unenjoyed, impairs our enjoyment of the good before us." Beyond our desire for possessions and pleasures, however, lies the still greater desire for simple fellowship, for the giving and receiving of assistance that "constitutes the happiness of human life." And he concludes by contrasting another Defoean solitary—an Indian in the wilderness—with the civilized inhabitants of London, whose life shows "how much society is to be desired" and how benevolent community can be.

Johnson's periodical essays sound this theme of benevolent community over and over; their phrases rally us like drumbeats to each other:

"the great republick of humanity" (*Rambler* 136)
"the great republick of mankind" (*Rambler* 81)

"the universal league of social beings" (*Rambler* 81)

"that tenderness and benevolence which by the privilege of their common nature one man may claim from another" (*Rambler* 145)

"The great end of society is mutual beneficence." (*Rambler* 56)

"The apparent insufficiency of every individual to his own happiness or safety, compels us to seek from one another assistance and support." (*Rambler* 104)

"the great community of the world" (*Rambler* 135)

"the great law of social beings, by which every individual is commanded to consult the happiness of others" (*Rambler* 148)

"Mankind is one vast republick, where every individual receives many benefits from the labour of others, which, by labouring in his turn for others, he is obliged to repay." (*Idler* 19)

The emphasis on individual helplessness in many of these quotations reminds us that Johnson's acute sensitivity to solitude, both personal and universal, strengthens his vision of our natural community. (And we remember how often he stresses the *narrowness* of life in the country as opposed to London.) But as W. J. Bate observes, "hardly any theme is single in Johnson."[37] Our drive for society against solitude necessarily creates a city of suffering: "It has been always considered as an alleviation of misery not to suffer alone, even when union and society can contribute nothing to resistance or escape" (*Rambler* 76). When the fictional characters of the essays are not alone in their vanity or distress, they face "the general hostility which every part of mankind exercises against the rest" (*Rambler* 173), the inevitable consequence of "the desire of many for that which only few can possess" (*Rambler* 183). Our thirst for self-importance thus tempts us to join in a second kind of community, the conspiratorial envy by which the human republic is so often dissolved. As Johnson touches upon this theme, we feel how close we are to the center of his deep, sympathetic melancholy. The divisions to which our common nature condemns us lie beneath and beyond all our partial ideas of community. "Every man must have remarked the facility with which the kindness of others is sometimes gained by those to whom he never could have imparted his own," Johnson writes with inexpressible sadness in *Rambler* 160.

> We are by our occupations, education and habits of life divided almost into different species, which regard one another for the most part with scorn and malignity. Each of these classes of the human race has desires, fears, and conversation, vexations and merriment peculiar to itself; cares which another cannot feel; pleasures which he cannot partake; and modes of expressing every sensation which he cannot understand.

Johnson comes finally to rest upon an assertion of our collectivity that subsumes community. He finds no pattern of encounter or relationship such as Dickens creates, only the shared fact of our innate condition, limited, impermanent, appalling.

The proper response to this perception is to trust in the hereafter and, in this world, to obey the great law of action. He prays for "love, which scarce collective man can fill," in *The Vanity of Human Wishes,* a love, as Bronson glosses, "so all-embracing that mankind will hardly suffice it; Christian, unselfish love, an 'obedient' passion."[38] And in practical terms he reminds us, by example as much as precept, of the charity we ought to practice. Johnson led a life of allegory, as Bate says.[39] In that enormous collection of human misery and interest, London, he clasped every opportunity for genuine benevolence. His strange household of misfits and invalids, his kindness to the city's wretched prostitutes, his quiet assistance to literary supplicants are quite as much a part of his character as the hectoring title of Doctor or Great Cham. I have sometimes wondered why Johnson never abandoned London for Oxford, where he loved the society of scholars and the atmosphere of venerable antiquity. London, of course, offered fame, challenge, distraction, which Johnson sought as desperately as anyone. But chiefly, one suspects, London serves as a correcting force for him—correcting the airiness and aridness of too intellectual or too retired a life. The city confronts him with men coarser than in the university—with Savages, Levets, Thrales—it provides fields of experience, not theory. Johnson's rootedness in London suggests the rootedness of his thought in the concrete, the living, the capacious as opposed to the simply academic and the cloistered. "The first time I was in company with Dr. Johnson," wrote Frances Reynolds years after his death, "I remember the impression I felt in his favour, on his saying that as he return'd to his lodgings about one or two o'clock in the morning, he often saw poor children asleep on thresholds and stalls, and that he used to put pennies into their hands to buy them a breakfast" (*JM*, II, 250–51). It is an unforgettable image of London—Johnson awkward and lonely moving through its darkened streets, past the ragged children cast up against its corners, bending in an act of charity more eloquent than any essay: a fully human city, actual but not unacceptable.

4

Wordsworth's London

In the summer of 1802 William Wordsworth left London in a very different mood from Juvenal's or Johnson's Thales. The poet and his sister Dorothy were on their way to France, to make final accommodations with his lover Annette Vallon and to see his child Caroline before his marriage to Mary Hutchinson. At Dover, before gaining shipboard, Dorothy recorded in her journal the first day's travel: "We left London on Saturday morning at half past five or six, the 30th [should be 31st] of July. We mounted the Dover coach at Charing Cross. It was a beautiful morning. The city, St. Paul's, with the river, and a multitude of little boats, made a most beautiful sight as we crossed Westminster Bridge. The houses were not over-hung by their cloud of smoke, and they were spread out endlessly, yet the sun shone so brightly, with such a fierce light, that there was something like the purity of one of nature's own grand spectacles" (*PW,* III, 431).[1] Wordsworth himself adds the further detail that they looked out at this grand spectacle from the roof of the coach; sometime during that morning he composed the most beautiful and best known portrait of London in our language.

> EARTH has not anything to show more fair:
> Dull would he be of soul who could pass by
> A sight so touching in its majesty:
> This City now doth, like a garment, wear
> The beauty of the morning; silent, bare,
> Ships, towers, domes, theatres, and temples lie
> Open unto the fields, and to the sky;

All bright and glittering in the smokeless air.
Never did sun more beautifully steep
In his first splendour, valley, rock, or hill;
Ne'er saw I, never felt, a calm so deep!
The river glideth at his own sweet will:
Dear God! the very houses seem asleep;
And all that mighty heart is lying still!

[*PW*, III, 38]

It is not London as we have been accustomed to see it—certainly not at the moment of leave-taking, when gestures of defiance or relief have been more common, like Wordsworth's own at the beginning of *The Prelude*—yet curiously his poem belongs to a lively minor eighteenth-century tradition of panoramic views from Westminster Bridge. A German visitor, Carl Moritz, sketched in 1786 a version of what Wordsworth must have seen:

The prospect from this bridge alone seems to afford one the epitome of a journey, or a voyage in miniature, as containing something of everything that most usually occurs on a journey. It is a little assemblage of contrasts and contrarieties. In contrast to the round, modern and majestic Cathedral of St. Paul's on your right, the venerable, old-fashioned, and hugely noble long Abbey of Westminster, with its enormous pointed roof, rises on the left. Down the Thames to the right you see Blackfriar's Bridge, which does not yield much, if at all, in beauty to that of Westminster; on the left bank of the Thames are beautiful terraces, planted with trees, and those new tasteful buildings called the Adelphi. On the Thames itself are countless swarms of little boats passing and repassing, many with one mast and one sail, and many with none, in which people of all ranks are carried over.[2]

And other writers confirmed the impressiveness of the sight, something of which can still be felt in Thomas Bowles's engraving of 1752.[3] His biographer, moreover, cites a view of London from Highgate Hill in John Thelwall's *Peripatetic* that Wordsworth may have recollected: "No sooner did I behold the vast metropolis expanding beneath my feet . . . see turrets, spires, and cupolas thronging in pompous vassalage round the still more magnificent dome, than wonder and delight rushed immediately to my heart. Nature—Nature perhaps was knocking at my bosom, and hard indeed must have been that heart that did not beat at the prospect of a place where it had so many inducements."[4] We can ourselves trace several familiar ways of seeing the city in Wordsworth's poem, particularly the imaging of London as a human body, clothed, beautiful, asleep, and with a heart. But the truth is that nothing in the setting, the tradition, or Wordsworth's reading accounts for the mysterious power of his vision. Even the concerns for the coming journey and the reunion with Annette Vallon, anxieties which had surely seized his attention, appear to leave no imprint upon the poem; and the other great sonnets of this summer—"It is a beauteous evening," "To Milton," "The world is too much with us"—have no clear connection with it either, except perhaps in their recurrent images of calm and freedom. Wordsworth seems always to have had the facility for ignoring in his poetry the pressures and events of the moment—"not used to make/A present joy the matter of a song," as he says at the beginning of *The Prelude.* We come upon the Westminster Bridge sonnet with much the same awed surprise that Wordsworth himself came upon this view of a city to him otherwise feverish and dreadful.[5]

Most readers have contented themselves with explaining the poem's effect by pointing toward the contrast upon which it is built. "London," as a midcentury observer succinctly put it, ". . . conveys no other idea but that of business and bustle."[6] Yet Wordsworth evokes for us another idea of the city altogether, here totally silent, free of movement, business, bustle; open—unfortified and vulnerable—and seemingly extending like a natural object itself "unto the fields, and to the sky." His is a London of absences and silences. Everyone has felt the fragility of a great city at such a moment, a fragility borne in upon us by the knowledge that its motionless beauty is about to be exchanged for energy; in Wordsworth's case stressed still further no doubt by the knowledge that he himself is embarking from it upon an unwanted voyage. His instinctual personification of the city captures exactly that sense of bravery we feel in the bare buildings and undisturbed river, and it captures also that momentary experience of personal relationship we enter into with what we know really to be an impersonal, indifferent creation.

Most readers will see this contrast as at the heart of the sonnet's meaning, adding perhaps the additional contrast between city and nature implied in it, which we more usually associate with Wordsworth. But some recent students have asked us to understand Wordsworth's poems generally, and the Westminster Bridge sonnet particularly, as built upon contrasts deeper still. David Ferry speaks of the tension, even "hostility," between surface and deeper meanings in his poetry: "It is often as if the 'surface' meanings of the poems were a beautiful and intelligible message, apparent at once, and as if hidden in that message there were clues to a 'deeper' meaning, still more beautiful though in some ways at odds with the message one had read at first."[7] From his point of view the last line of the poem, scrupulously read, reveals the deeper meaning that Wordsworth unconsciously withholds:

> And all that mighty heart is lying still!

"The city is not merely sleeping, but dead, its heart stilled. The poet looks at London and sees it as a sort of corpse and admires it as such, welcomes a death which is the death of what the city has come to stand for in his symbolic world"— that is, the common passions of all ordinary urban life, which repel and frighten Wordsworth and move in opposition to the permanence or eternality he seeks as poet.[8] We look upon Wordsworth's London here, in other words, as we gaze upon Odilon Redon's beautiful paintings of flowers, which after study come to seem to us not only beautiful, but poisonous. This way of reading the poem enlarges its significance, though at a cost, and links it to Wordsworth's other denunciations of London; it confirms the rightness of the teacher's habit of placing this poem beside Blake's "London" as an exercise in comparison, for Blake's great poem, an unambiguous attack

upon the city, is fully, if mysteriously matched by Wordsworth's admiring sonnet; and yet the careful reader can see
that his poem attacks, however obliquely, the same things.
But even if we accept them, the two meanings of Wordsworth's poem that Ferry discerns do not simply alternate in
the reader's mind after the manner of Augustan irony, like
E. H. Gombrich's drawing of the rabbit/duck. Most readers
would agree that the two meanings—the frail, haunting city,
and the corpse of it—exist inseparably, simultaneously if at
all; we somehow look *through* the first meaning to the second,
but without for a moment relinquishing either, certainly
without relinquishing the loveliness that first draws the poet's
eye. The poem, finally, may be understood by us to occupy
something like the same position in Wordsworth's work as
Windsor-Forest does in Pope's, for despite all subtlety it can
nonetheless stand as one version of a holy city, one whose
living river and panorama of ships, towers, domes, theaters,
and temples belong to the very earliest ways of celebrating
an ideal London.

I

Already at three stages' distance (say, 40 miles from London), upon some of the greatest roads, the dim presenti-
ment of some vast capital reaches you obscurely, and like
a misgiving. This blind sympathy with a mighty but unseen object, some vast magnetic range of Alps, in your
neighbourhood, continues to increase, you know not
how. Arrived at the last station for changing horses,—
Barnet, suppose, on one of the north roads, or Hounslow
on the western,—you no longer think (as in all other
places) of naming the next stage; nobody says, on pulling
up, "Horses on to London"; that would sound ridiculous;
one mighty idea broods over all minds, making it impossible to suppose any other destination. Launched upon
this final stage, you soon begin to feel yourself entering
the stream as it were of a Norwegian *maelstrom;* and the
stream at length becomes the rush of a cataract.[9]

Thomas De Quincey's account of his first visit to London, the chapter in his *Autobiography* called "The Nation of London," sets up impossible expectations. Nothing in life could embody the mighty idea of the city that attracts him, nothing in time could approach the abiding force of a London at once Alp and maelstrom, cataract and magnet. Before his experience begins, his imagination has subverted it: we are hardly surprised to hear him complaining upon arrival of the shortness of time he has for touring—"our very wealth made us poor"—what sight "could be thought general or representative enough to stand for the universe of London?" And the vast capital joins other examples of disappointment he has felt in the presence of places and events he has *known* to be great: a painting of Cape Horn, the coronation of George IV, and (most appropriate for London) the farewell performance of David Garrick. De Quincey is willing to explain such disappointments in terms of disproportion and impermanence— "the incongruity of any audience . . . to any purpose less evanescent than their own tenure of existence"—but it will not do damage to his explanation, I think, if we add that his insatiable anticipation, of London, of Cape Horn, of whatever, is a species of Romantic idealism. The sensibility of the observer devours the mundane realities of a life that flickers through uneven, imperfect moments; De Quincey's brooding London quickly collapses into streets, buildings, persons, and impertinences. By contrast, the London Pope holds up as Augusta exists as part of a long series of civilizing ideals, linked to a permanent past that stretches backward toward Rome and Troy; the disappointments his London inflicts also spring from a failure of ideal, but the failure lies with the Dunces and the times, not with the audience that watches, least of all with the irreversible fact of their evanescent existence. De Quincey's stages to London are traveled in a new spirit, one less openly exhibitionistic than Boswell's, for example, but far more deeply committed to an egoism that will give way grudgingly, bitterly, to the harsh indifference of the city. Characteristically, and like every writer on the city after him, he turns to the theme of self-conscious loneliness: "you become aware that you are no longer noticed; nobody sees you; nobody hears you; nobody regards you; you do not even regard yourself. In fact, how should you at the moment of first ascertaining your own total unimportance in the sum of things—a poor, shivering unit in the aggregate of human life?" The sensibility of the observer is unequal to the experience. "No loneliness can be like that which weighs upon the heart in the centre of faces never-ending, without voice or utterance for him; eyes innumerable, that have 'no speculation' in their orbs which *he* can understand; and hurrying figures of men and women weaving to and fro, with no apparent purposes intelligible to a stranger, seeming like a mask of maniacs, or, oftentimes, like a pageant of phantoms." From the perspective of Pope, Defoe, and even Johnson, it is a new London, and a new failure.

Wordsworth comes to London in a spirit like De Quincey's. Book VII of *The Prelude,* substantially composed in the late autumn of 1804, begins with two waves of expectation: the first describing the poet's resumption of work after a summer of inactivity and distraction, the second describing the rich images of far-off London he held as a child. The opening lines of the book, moreover, recall the first lines of *The Prelude* itself, when he had "escaped/From the vast city" and briefly "sang/Aloud, with fervour irresistible" until his inspiration vanished. Now a choir of robins near his cottage seem

> minstrels from the distant woods
> Sent in on Winter's service, to announce
> With preparation artful and benign,
> That the rough lord had left the surly North
> On his accustomed journey.
> [VII, 22–26][10]

And the excitement of poetry intimated but not yet audible rises in him:

> I in whispers said,
> "Ye heartsome Choristers, ye and I will be
> Associates, and, unscared by blustering winds,
> Will chant together."
> [VII, 29–31]

Never has Wordsworth seemed closer to Nature, her songs and his echo and blend; he turns as in book I to the favorite image of a correspondent breeze.

> The last night's genial feeling overflowed
> Upon this morning, and my favourite grove,
> Tossing in sunshine its dark boughs aloft,
> As if to make the strong wind visible,
> Wakes in me agitations like its own,
> A spirit friendly to the Poet's task,
> Which we will now resume with lively hope,
> Nor checked by aught of tamer argument
> That lies before us, needful to be told.
>
> [VII, 43–51]

But ironically these beautiful natural powers must now serve the needful argument of city life, London and all its artificial, man-made agitations.

A phrase from the preceding book of *The Prelude* will occur to many readers as they make their way through Wordsworth's second invocation of anticipated powers, his first distant impressions of London. In book VI he had told how, after many days of travel, he and his friend had at last glimpsed the very peak of Mont Blanc, thus far seen only in their imaginations, when to their surprise they discovered that they

> grieved
> To have a soulless image on the eye
> that had usurped upon a living thought
> That never more could be.
>
> [VI, 525–28]

But the Vale of Chamouny stretching beneath the mountain displaces the sense of anticlimax, and memorably he confesses that

> A motionless array of mighty waves,
> Five rivers broad and vast, made rich amends,
> And reconciled us to realities.
>
> [VI, 531–33]

It is a profound tribute to the "realities" of nature, their ability to keep pace with his imagination, or almost to keep pace; and it reveals too that dark tension which Geoffrey Hartman has seen at the center of Wordsworth's poetry, the impulse he feels toward visionary poetry like Blake's, but which he evades by anchoring his vision stubbornly in natural forms.[11] Wordsworth begins the story of his residence in London with a similar "living thought"—what De Quincey called the mighty idea of London—as yet unviolated by experience:

> There was a time when whatso'er is feigned
> Of airy palaces, and gardens built
> By Genii of romance; or hath in grave
> Authentic history been set forth of Rome,
> Alcairo, Babylon, or Persepolis;
> Or given upon report by pilgrim friars,
> Of golden cities ten months' journey deep
> Among Tartarian wilds—fell short, far short,
> Of what my fond simplicity believed
> And thought of London—held me by a chain
> Less strong of wonder and obscure delight.
>
> [VII, 77–87]

The first line echoes the opening of the Immortality Ode, and the echo prepares us for the theme of loss that is inevitably to follow; "feigned" (and "childhood's Fancy" in line 88) likewise prepares us for disappointment and, together with comparisons to the fabulous palaces of romances or ancient history, at the same time quietly associates the city and the idea of illusion. The list of unequal predecessors— Rome, Alcairo, Babylon—alludes, ominously, to lines in *Paradise Lost* describing Satan's palace in Hell:

> not *Babylon*,
> Nor great *Alcairo* such magnificence
> Equall'd in all thir glories. . . .
>
> [I, 717–19]

Even before this introductory passage Wordsworth has begun

to darken his portrait of London. The paragraph recounting
his decision to come to the city after his term at Cambridge
(VII, 58–76) insists upon its unmanageable size, the "shock"
of its presence, its incessant whirls of traffic and Pleasure.
Now his youthful fantasy "Of mitred Prelates, Lords in
ermine clad,/The King, and the King's Palace" is deflated by
the report of a schoolmate who has visited the city and re-
turned somehow unchanged, although "as if from Fairy-land."

> Much I questioned him;
> And every word he uttered, on my ears
> Fell flatter than a cagèd parrot's note,
> That answers unexpectedly awry,
> And mocks the prompter's listening.
>   [VII, 98–102]

One disenchantment is succeeded by a second, far more unsettling:

> Above all, one thought
> Baffled my understanding: how men lived
> Even next-door neighbours, as we say, yet still
> Strangers, not knowing each the other's name.
>   [VII, 115–18]

The unaccountable discrepancy between his "Dreams" (VII,
111) of London and its realities pushes him, as it did De
Quincey, toward the same theme of alienation in the city.
These unacquainted neighbors are not to be mistaken for
Wordsworthian solitaries, impressive figures like the Leech-
Gatherer who stand apart from other men, but who are not
unrelated to them; these strangers are alienated from each
other at the most basic level of language: their names, their
identities. Adumbrated here—and shortly to be made explicit—is a view of urban chaos to be set beside Pope's. But
whereas in Pope's London, the Dunces simply rage through a
landscape of streets and buildings, united at least by their
destructive energy, Wordsworth expresses a different consciousness of disorder. The image of noncommunication we
see in the questioner and the caged parrot now swells into a

city of random, unattached lives, a dream more inconceivable
than any Genii of romance.

I dwell thus long upon the opening section of book VII
because it compresses in a convenient space most of the
concerns that shape the remainder of the book. Illusion,
communication, chaotic movement—these ideas will be
embodied in concrete images of theater, language, and festival and unified by a vision of London that stresses, in a recognizably modern way, its irritating, tragic insufficiencies.

II

At his leisure, Wordsworth tells us, he surveyed the spectacles of London, the birds, animals, plants and people that
the great city collected from over the globe. Especially, he
says in a phrase still more striking than the "reconciled us to
realities" of Mont Blanc, he delighted in

> those sights that ape
> The absolute presence of reality,
> Expressing, as in mirror, sea and land,
> And what earth is, and what she has to shew.
> [VII, 232–35]

He means, of course, the paintings, statues, and models to be
found everywhere in London ("The arts," as William Empson
remarks, "are produced by overcrowding"),[12] but his language
contains an unusual pressure. The paintings he finds on the
streets and in the shops fall short of experienced reality—"ape"
it—and yet so long as they faithfully represent natural forms
of sea and land and earth his tone remains forgiving, toler-
antly approving:

> I do not here allude to subtlest craft,
> By means refined attaining purest ends,
> But imitations, fondly made in plain
> Confession of man's weakness and his loves.
> [VII, 236–39]

The "purest ends" of art have plainly some larger moral
force behind them than these simple imitations; but such

genuine art will only be refined from this initial, healthy impulse to mirror and halt the world around us.

Paintings and sculptures, however, are merely "exhibitions, mute and still" (VII, 260). The city displays its more characteristic art in exhibitions that move and shift, in pantomimes and dances, and above all in the theater. The playhouses obviously enchanted Wordsworth as a young man—nothing else in the vast capital approached his boyhood dreams of a London "Fairy-land," and he haunted every kind of performance the city offered, from the crude shows of clowns and conjurers in the streets or at "Half-rural Sadler's Wells" (VII, 267) to the slick pageants of Drury Lane. Like one of Pope's uncritical mobsters in the pit—recollected in "many-headed mass/Of the spectators" (VII, 434–35)—he seems to have responded chiefly to the theater's appearances, applauding the "ever-shifting figures of the scene" (VII, 412) and relishing the gorgeous costumes of the actors. (The same taste is apparent in his long account of the exotic foreigners he sees in the city.) He recalls nothing of the drama, only its effects:

> whether some beauteous dame
> Advanced in radiance through a deep recess
> Of thick entangled forest, like the moon
> Opening the clouds; or sovereign king, announced
> With flourishing trumpet, came in full-blown state
> Of the world's greatness, winding round with train
> Of courtiers, banners, and a length of guards.
>   [VII, 413–19]

And yet indispensable to this pleasure, which he compares to the liveliness of a kitten at play, is the knowledge that the theater's surface of illusion is penetrable, that there is no aspiration here toward absolute reality. He joins London stage and boyhood countryside through a memory of just such conscious penetration:

> When at a country-playhouse, some rude barn
> Tricked out for that proud use, if I perchance
> Caught, on a summer evening through a chink
> In the old wall, an unexpected glimpse
> Of daylight, the bare thought of where I was

Gladdened me more than if I had been led
Into a dazzling cavern of romance,
Crowded with Genii. . . .

[VII, 449–56]

And our impression of innocence is completed by his reversion
to the childhood Genii and romances of book VII's opening.

A very different memory, of corruption rather than self-
consciousness, also links theater and countryside, but changes
Wordsworth's theme from theatrical illusion to moral deceit.
The Maid of Buttermere, a native of his own region, had become the subject of a melodrama he attended at Sadler's
Wells in 1802: the sentimental story of an "artless daughter
of the hills" (VII, 300) and a city-bred "spoiler" who biga-
mously married and deserted her. Wordsworth pays a pious,
saccharine tribute to her virtues and prepares to leave the
subject, when suddenly—he cannot say why—it rises like
Imagination from "the mind's abyss" in book VI and insists
upon elaboration: "thy image rose again,/Maiden of Buttermere!" (VII, 319–20). Yet what he now recalls is not the
woman but the child she bore, who "Beside the mountain
chapel, sleeps in earth/Her new-born infant, fearless as a
lamb" (VII, 324–25). And his mind then ducks once more
to London and the memory of "a lovely Boy" and dissolute
mother, a prostitute, whom he had once seen at the theater.
The boy seemed "A sort of alien scattered from the clouds"
(VII, 350)—a "cottage-child"—and in a striking passage he
describes how

Upon a board
Decked with refreshments had this child been placed,
His little stage in the vast theatre,
And there he sate surrounded with a throng
Of chance spectators, chiefly dissolute men
And shameless women, treated and caressed;
Ate, drank, and with the fruit and glasses played,
While oaths and laughter and indecent speech
Were rife about him as the songs of birds
Contending after showers.

[VII, 356–65]

We may be reminded of Marina among the whores in Shakespeare's *Pericles,* or of Clarissa Harlowe in Mrs. Sinclair's brothel: the image is of an unworldly virtue that somehow survives the abrasions of a wicked, ordinary life. But Wordsworth has created a context—or followed an association—that makes the dissoluteness specifically a consequence of city life. The scene is illuminated by the "glare/From playhouse lustres," the mother's "tints" are "False," the boy's admirers merely "chance spectators," his stage set against the cottage or "sheltering vale" that ought to be his by right, by nature. A new comparison transforms the stage lights into the glow of Nebuchadnezzar's oven, where Shadrach, Meshak, and Abednego walked unharmed:

> I see
> The lovely Boy as I beheld him then
> Among the wretched and the falsely gay,
> Like one of those who walked with hair unsinged
> Amid the fiery furnace.
>
> [VII, 366–70]

Wordsworth's metamorphosis of the city here might well call to mind his earlier allusions to Milton's Hell—for which the fiery furnace is an Old Testament type—but the poet's images now push even further toward the meaning that has lain hidden in the story of the Maid. Charms have sometimes been used to frustrate "kindliest growths." He questions:

> Ah, with how different spirit might a prayer
> Have been preferred, that this fair creature, checked
> By special privilege of Nature's love,
> Should in his childhood be detained forever!
>
> [VII, 373–76]

This passage may seem to us syntactically contorted, evasively wordy, as if Wordsworth wishes to avoid its implications. In 1805 he had written more directly, but with the shocking word "embalmed," that

> He hath since
> Appear'd to me oft-times as if embalm'd

> By Nature; through some special privilege,
> Stopp'd at the growth he had.
>
> [VII, 398–401]

In both versions he places the boy alongside the Maid's child and imagines a look of envy for the "nameless babe that sleeps,/Beside the mountain chapel, undisturbed" (VII, 380–81).

Mother, child, and death; Nature that embalms and loves— these conjunctions lie at the heart of the Wordsworthian mystery. The drive for fame in Johnson's London has given way to the search for absolute integrity that Wordsworth instinctively pursues apart from the city. Every reader will sense how deeply he identifies his own childhood with the Maid and her son, and how the prayer for death is intended to check the loss that any growth in time—any expectation— accomplishes. But from our present point of view it is enough to say that the image of the city as mother that we saw in the *Dunciad* has reappeared (and again less obviously in lines like "true epitome/Of what the mighty City is herself/To thousands upon thousands of her sons" [VII, 722–24]). Wordsworth has not joined London and the river Thames to form an archetypal maternal figure as Pope did, but like Pope he creates a mother who presides over an urban scene of folly and neglect. When we remember Pope's Dulness exhorting her bawdy flock of Dunces to their games in Fleet Ditch, the difference in tone between his conception and Wordsworth's is more than apparent: Pope's "mighty mother" storms the city, demonic, unforgivable, a living principle of disorder, while the mother of the Lovely Boy sits almost unnoticed in the crowd; aside from the lurid detail of her false tints, she has faded from his memory, and Wordsworth dismisses her in a voice sympathetic and unremonstrating. But opposites though they be in energy, both mothers are presented as authentic daughters of Babylon. In their presence it is impossible not to be reminded of yet another eighteenth-century image of motherhood and London, the closing lines of Blake's "London," where the "youthful Harlots curse," the "new-born Infants tears," and the "charter'd Thames" make the same litany of denunciation. And all three poems move toward the same end: Pope invokes Niobe and Hecuba, Blake "the Marriage hearse," and Wordsworth the "embalm'd," dead child of his wishful imagination. In *The Prelude* one further image is added. The mother of the Lovely Boy no more than parodies the Maid of Buttermere, who lives "without contamination" but whose son sleeps in earth beside the mountain chapel: the good mother gives her child up to an early, embracing death, but the bad sets him to live undetained, in both time and the city.

   The incident of the Maid of Buttermere belongs in a general way to a long European tradition of attack upon the immorality of the stage, a genre that frequently spills over into an attack upon the city. Jean Jacques Rousseau, to take one example, habitually identifies theater and civic corruption; and in the *Lettre à M. d'Alembert* he argues that the introduction of a playhouse into his pleasant countryside (especially the introduction of actresses) will subvert the morality of country girls ("timide et modeste . . . elles n'osent [pas] lever les yeux sur les hommes, et gardent le silence devant eux") and that luxury, taxation, laziness—every kind of vice inevitably will follow.[13] A countertradition, represented conveniently by Boswell and later by Charles Lamb, mounts a vigorous defense on occasion, quite as frequently in the context of a celebration of the city: "I have no hesitation in declaring," Lamb says, in an essay called "The Londoner," "that a mob of happy faces crowding up at the pit door of Drury-lane Theatre, just at the hour of six, gives me ten thousand sincerer plesures, than I could ever receive from all the flocks of silly sheep that ever whitened the plains of Arcadia or Epsom Downs." And praising the effects of busy streets upon his spirit, he automatically applies the metaphor of theater: "Often, when I have felt a weariness or distaste at home, have I rushed out into her crowded Strand, and fed my humour, till tears have wetted my cheek for unutterable sympathies with the multitudinous moving picture, which she never fails to present at all hours, like the scenes of a shifting pantomime."[14] Wordsworth's position at first glance appears ambiguous. He has no classical standards for the drama, as Pope does, from which the modern age knavishly departs; he draws no overt moral from the boy's "little stage in the vast theatre"; he makes no mention, as we might expect, of the insincerity of acting, which is a constant provocation to Rousseau and others. And yet his London is ultimately felt to be suffused with theatricality, heaving with it as if in a fever, trapped in a constant whirl of illusion and unnaturalness. "Trivial" is the word he most often uses for this quality of London life, its appetite for meaningless distraction, and in opposition he places untheatrical "realities." For despite his pleasure in all the trappings of the playhouse, he reports, the "imaginative power" languished within him. He makes a startling urban metaphor of his mind, only to discover that

> though I was most passionately moved
> And yielded to all changes of the scene
> With an obsequious promptness, yet the storm
> Passed not beyond the suburbs of the mind;
> Save when realities of act and mien,
> The incarnations of the spirits that move
> In harmony amid the Poet's world,
> Rose to ideal grandeur.
>
> [VII, 473–80]

The extraordinary portrait of Bartholomew Fair with which book VII concludes, and to which we must shortly turn, is the fullest expression of this imaginative sleep; but the story of the Maid of Buttermere raises one other theme that we have encountered earlier.

III

Like Pope, Wordsworth makes language an artifact of urbanity. He turns from the story of the Maid of Buttermere to recall how, "travelling southward from our pastoral hills," for the first time in his life he had heard

> The voice of woman utter blasphemy—
> Saw woman as she is, to open shame

> Abandoned, and the pride of public vice;
> I shuddered, for a barrier seemed at once
> Thrown in, that from humanity divorced
> Humanity, splitting the race of man
> In twain, yet leaving the same outward form.
>   [VII, 385–91]

This is the language of corruption that Pope also found in the city (we may be reminded of Dulness's "Bawdry, Bilingsgate, my daughters dear"), and it too is juxtaposed with ideas of perverse motherhood and death, just as in the *Dunciad.* But Wordsworth's feeling for the relationship between London and language is less sweeping than Pope's, and less urgent. The disintegration of standards that Pope sees as part of the fate of Dultown, the disorderly language that emblematizes the disorderly city are not concerns that deeply touch him. Wordsworth senses the role that speech plays in creating the city around him—like every observer he talks of "the Babel din," the "female vendor's scream, belike/The very shrillest of all London cries" (VII, 182–83), the rumble of traffic—yet his response goes less to the fact of discord than to the fact of deception. The blasphemous prostitute disturbs him in large part because, like Spenser's Duessa, her outward form appears to him virtuous, but her reality is shameless and unhuman. For him the strain placed by the city upon language leads, as the image of the theater did, to questions of illusion and reality, expectation and reconciliation.

The introductory section of book VII concludes with Wordsworth's puzzlement at the report of neighbors in the city "not knowing each the other's name." Then an unexpected outburst:

> O, wond'rous power of words, by simple faith
> Licensed to take the meaning that we love!
> Vauxhall and Ranelagh! I then had heard
> Of your green groves, and wilderness of lamps
> Dimming the stars, and fireworks magical,
> And gorgeous ladies, under splendid domes,

> Floating in dance, or warbling high in air
> The songs of spirits!
>
> [VII, 119–26]

Vauxhall and Ranelagh, famous pleasure gardens outside London where in season the fashionable world dined and promenaded, belong to the class of spectacles, more or less theatrical, in which Wordsworth then delighted. The other "marvels" of the city that he goes on to name—St. Paul's, Westminster, Guildhall, Bedlam—were likewise once "bold imaginations," but experience has faded all of them into familiarity; only a simple faith in language triggers them back into fresh meaning.

In the 1805 version of the poem this consideration of the creating—not uncreating power—of words to build a city is followed by a demonstration: a long, detailed account of a day's walk through London streets according to the model of Gay's *Trivia*.

> The endless stream of men, and moving things,
> From hour to hour the illimitable walk
> Still among Streets with clouds and sky above,
> The wealth, the bustle and the eagerness,
> The glittering Chariots with their pamper'd Steeds,
> Stalls, Barrows, Porters; midway in the Street
> The Scavenger, who begs with hat in hand,
> The labouring Hackney Coaches, the rash speed
> Of Coaches travelling far . . .
>
> [VII, 158–66]

And so on, as the poet weaves in and out of byways, private courts, and throngs until we turn homeward and to the subject of theater and painting. Much of the tour was retained in 1850, but one significant addition, changing the tone abruptly from reminiscence to disapproval, places a familiar image for the city beside the motif of language:

> Rise up, thou monstrous ant-hill on the plain
> Of a too busy world! Before me flow,

Thou endless stream of men and moving things!
Thy every-day appearance, as it strikes—
With wonder heightened, or sublimed by awe—
On strangers of all ages; the quick dance
Of colours, lights, and forms; the deafening din;
The comers and the goers face to face,
Face after face; the string of dazzling wares,
Shop after shop, with symbols, blazoned names,
And all the trademan's honours overhead:
Here, fronts of houses, like a title-page,
With letters huge inscribed from top to toe,
Stationed above the door, like guardian saints;
There, allegoric shapes, female or male,
Or physiognomies of real men,
Land-warriors, kings, or admirals of the sea,
Boyle, Shakespeare, Newton, or the attractive head
Of some quack-doctor, famous in his day.

[VII, 149–67]

It is one of Wordsworth's few references to trade in London,
the staple of Defoe, but our attention is drawn away from
shops and businesses first to the "monstrous ant-hill" rising
and then to the transformation of city into written language:
the "fronts of houses, like a title-page,/With letters huge inscribed" becoming finally the famous "allegoric" street signs.
The anthill is the reverse of Pope's and Mandeville's hive:
monstrous, it gives little sense of the collective life of the
city, only its endless movement, a "quick dance" carried on
by the abstractions of colors, lights, and forms. And yet in an
apparently haphazard way these forms resolve into human
beings—"The comers and the goers face to face,/Face after
face"—and next into language. J. Hillis Miller has noted how
frequently Wordsworth personifies nature as a human body,
"and in particular as an expressive and speaking face."[15] The
attentive reader of book VII may be reminded by the transi-
tion here from faces to symbols of a great moment in book
VI that combines face and language into a metaphor and that
also follows a description of sublime and turbulent disorder:

The torrents shooting from the clear blue sky,
The rocks that muttered close upon our ears,
Black drizzling crags that spake by the way-side
As if a voice were in them, the sick sight
And giddy prospect of the raving stream,
The unfettered clouds and region of the Heavens,
Tumult and peace, the darkness and the light—
Were all like workings of one mind, the features
Of the same face, blossoms upon one tree;
Characters of the great Apocalypse,
The types and symbols of Eternity,
Of first, and last, and midst, and without end.

[VI, 629–40]

We feel in book VII the dynamics of Wordsworth's habitual
approach to nature, now applied to London: he verges upon
a personification of the city comparable to the one he con-
structs for the Alps, where voice, characters, types, symbols
are united into a single awe-inspiring face. His expectations
for the city are like his expectations for the mountains, he
proceeds to write about them in the same way; and yet in
London he falls back, unsuccessful, from either the impulse
or the attempt. The stress upon disappearance and emergence
from the city's "sequestered nooks" in the succeeding lines—
particularly the "labyrinths" that lead "to privileged regions
and inviolate"—adds to our sense of retreat and hesitation.
The labyrinth is the inside of the hive or anthill, the privileged
regions are internal, like the mind of the Apocalypse; but the
construction remains incomplete, and Wordsworth fails to
grasp some essential element of what he is describing, fails to
compress his perceptions into a metaphor of sublimity: no
face appears. His description of London trails out across its
streets and alleys toward the "files of ballads" dangling
"from dead walls" in the suburbs:

Advertisements, of giant-size, from high
Press forward, in all colours, on the sight;
These, bold in conscious merit, lower down;

> *That,* fronted with a most imposing word,
> Is, peradventure, one in masquerade.
>
> [VII, 194–98]

A second recollection of the city calls forth the same sequence of anticipation and internalization, and the same
imagery of labyrinths and language. In book VIII Wordsworth
recalls his first entrance into London:

> But how could I in mood so light indulge,
> Keeping such fresh remembrance of the day,
> When, having thridded the long labyrinth
> Of the suburban villages, I first
> Entered thy vast dominion? On the roof
> Of an itinerant vehicle I sate,
> With vulgar men about me, trivial forms
> Of houses, pavement, streets, of men and things,—
> Mean shapes on every side. . . .
>
> [VIII, 539–47]

The direction is inward. We push through "the long labyrinth"
toward the familiar whirl of "trivial forms," "Mean shapes";
and as in the Simplon Pass episode, when the knowledge that
he has crossed the Alps plunges him into disappointment,
here the knowledge that he has passed the "threshold" into
London sinks his spirits like a plummet:

>   but, at the instant,
> When to myself it fairly might be said,
> The threshold now is overpast, (how strange
> That aught external to the living mind
> Should have such mighty sway! yet so it was),
> A weight of ages did at once descend
> Upon my heart; no thought embodied, no
> Distinct remembrances, but weight and power,—
> Power growing under weight. . . .
>
> [VIII, 547–55]

A self-conscious comment—"alas! I feel/That I am trifling: 't
was a moment's pause"—is limply bolstered by assertion of
the moment's power: "yet with Time it dwells,/And grateful

memory, as a thing divine." And again as in the Simplon Pass, a deliberate image of sublimity is constructed, one which takes us from labyrinth to cavern, and from cavern to language.

> The curious traveller, who, from open day,
> Hath passed with torches into some huge cave,
> The Grotto of Antiparos, or the Den
> In old time haunted by that Danish Witch
> Yordas; he looks around and sees the vault
> Widening on all sides; sees, or thinks he sees,
> Erelong, the massy roof above his head,
> That instantly unsettles and recedes,—
> Substance and shadow, light and darkness, all
> Commingled, making up a canopy
> Of shapes and forms and tendencies to shape
> That shift and vanish, change and interchange
> Like spectres,—ferment silent and sublime!
> That after a short space works less and less,
> Till, every effort, every motion gone,
> The scene before him stands in perfect view
> Exposed, and lifeless as a written book!
>
> [VIII, 560–76]

The elements are all present—the commingling of "Substance and shadow, light and darkness," the great object, the observer, the summarizing metaphor—but few readers can feel that this spectral cavern comes near in poetic power to the one mind and face of Simplon Pass. The simile is forced, a little tiresome, even self-defeating: after a few moments, Wordsworth oddly confesses, the scene before the traveler subsides and "stands in perfect view/Exposed, and lifeless as a written book!" The cavern, like others in *The Prelude,* symbolizes the inward workings of the mind, a recess of creativity; but compared to the mind that unifies the mountain setting, it works to no purpose and creates, not "types and symbols of Eternity," but lifeless, unimportant "shapes." Almost as if he sensed this infertility, Wordsworth begins the metaphor once more:

> But let him pause awhile, and look again,

> And a new quickening shall succeed, at first
> Beginning timidly, then creeping fast,
> Till the whole cave, so late a senseless mass,
> Busies the eye with images and forms
> Boldly assembled,—here is shadowed forth
> From the projections, wrinkles, cavities,
> A variegated landscape,—there the shape
> Of some gigantic warrior clad in mail,
> The ghostly semblance of a hooded monk,
> Veiled nun, or pilgrim resting on his staff:
> Strange congregation! yet not slow to meet
> Eyes that perceive through minds that can inspire.
>
> [VIII, 577–89]

"Boldly assembled" now are figures from romance or theater, apparitions from a costume drama, unrelated to the cityscape with which this passage took its start. The poet pauses to affirm that his subject has been (as it has so often) the interaction of mind and external world—"Eyes that perceive through minds that can inspire"—and moves quickly on toward other matters.

Why has London failed to inspire him to sublimity, as the Alps had or Mount Snowdon afterward? Herbert Lindenberger has observed that Wordsworth's imagination requires motion like that of wind and water to awaken it; the "soulless image" of Mont Blanc, the immovable mountains "seem remote and solid entities, without direct contact with man or the natural elements"; "something final and dead about" them is the source of Wordsworth's disappointment.[16] Only the surrounding streams of water and mist and the blasts of icy wind make possible his saving, symbolizing interaction. London would appear to meet this indispensable requirement—no one has stressed more than Wordsworth the constant flow and stream (to use his necessary image) of life on its streets, the "tide" and "quick dance" of sight and sound—and yet his imagination awakens in the city only to withdraw. Hence the elaborate isolation of his "huge cave," the memories of distant nature that come to him in the midst of crowds. One other element, as Edmund Burke had long ago pointed out, is necessary for sublimity: the feeling of terror without real danger. The narrow, surreal Pass, the dizzying view downward from Mont Blanc—these and dozens of similar moments in Wordsworth's poetry serve his imagination by the fear, however groundless, they inspire. They permit relationship, metamorphosis, metaphor. And they permit one further thing. The craggy mountain peak that in book I of *The Prelude* seems to pursue the boy in his stolen boat looms up like angry conscience, "As if with voluntary power instinct"; and afterward

> for many days, my brain
> Worked with a dim and undetermined sense
> Of unknown modes of being; o'er my thoughts
> There hung a darkness, call it solitude
> Or blank desertion. No familiar shapes
> Remained, no pleasant images of trees,
> Of sea or sky, no colours of green fields;
> But huge and mighty forms, that do not live
> Like living men, mov'd slowly through the mind
> By day, and were a trouble to my dreams.
>
> [I, 391–400]

What Wordsworth finds in these "huge and mighty forms, that do not live/Like living men" is the knowledge—a gift to him like grace—"Of unknown modes of being." London is unendangering and trivial: its life is human, it lives like living men, its otherness is sameness to the philosophic mind.

IV

This single moment from book VII meets the conditions of sublimity:

> As the black storm upon the mountain top
> Sets off the sunbeam in the valley, so
> That huge fermenting mass of human-kind
> Serves as a solemn back-ground, or relief,
> To single forms and objects, whence they draw,
> For feeling and contemplative regard,
> More than inherent liveliness and power.

How oft, amid those overflowing streets,
Have I gone forward with the crowd, and said
Unto myself, "The face of every one
That passes by me is a mystery!"
Thus have I looked, nor ceased to look, oppressed
By thoughts of what and whither, when and how,
Until the shapes before my eyes became
A second-sight procession, such as glides
Over still mountains, or appears in dreams;
And once, far-travelled in such mood, beyond
The reach of common indication, lost
Amid the moving pageant, I was smitten
Abruptly, with the view (a sight not rare)
Of a blind Beggar, who, with upright face,
Stood, propped against a wall, upon his chest
Wearing a written paper, to explain
His story, whence he came, and who he was.
Caught by the spectacle my mind turned round
As with the might of waters; an apt type
This label seemed of the utmost we can know,
Both of ourselves and of the universe;
And, on the shape of that unmoving man,
His steadfast face and sightless eyes, I gazed,
As if admonished from another world.

[VII, 619–49]

Human, yet from another world; unmoving, yet in the "over-flowing streets"; admonishing, yet silent; mysterious, yet "Wearing a written paper, to explain/His story"—the Blind Beggar draws Wordsworth to his unknown mode of being. Confronted with such figures, in his *Essay on Charity and Charity Schools* Mandeville coolly analyzes the impatient pity of those who pass by and thinks how inevitable are beggars in a city; in a sentimental moment Lamb finds them endearing, part of the London scene.[17] But the Blind Beggar takes Wordsworth out of the illusory theater of the city's "moving pageant." The "solemn back-ground, or relief" from nature—sunbeam against storm—is insistently unurban; the crowds become a hypnotic "second-sight procession, such as glides/Over still mountains, or appears in dreams." What finally captures Wordsworth's alienated attention is first the beggar's distinctive solitude, his "upright face," and next the label that he wears upon his chest. Geoffrey Hartman has analyzed the essential identification we feel between label and face:

> These natural foci of any observer are shocking here because they are *not* in contrast. Face and label are equally fixed or affixed: we expect the beggar's face and eyes ("his steadfast face and sightless eyes") to be centers of life whereas they are as much a surface as the paper he wears. As in the central episode of the sixth book, it is both a mental anticipation and the expectation of a strongly visual significance which is defeated, and this again causes a quasi-apocalyptic feeling of reversal turning the mind round or into itself.[18]

We may add that neither label nor face has a specific content; the beggar's story and the poet's interpretation are beyond us. This written paper is both like and unlike the other label worn in book VII, the word "Invisible" pinned to the chest of Jack the Giantkiller in a play at Sadler's Wells: like, because it tells us who and what he is and hangs upon a symbolic background "black as death"; unlike, because it tells us, not the simple information of unself-consciousness, but rather "the utmost we can know,/Both of ourselves and of the universe." And while the label shows us the extremes of defeat in London, it also carries us back to the natural world where the features of one face are reexpressed in images of language: "Characters of the great Apocalypse,/The types and symbols of Eternity" (VI, 638–39). Like the love of the brawny Artificer for his sickly child, another sight Wordsworth remembers from the city, the meaning of the beggar's label is profoundly felt, but in the end "unutterable."

Because it occurs so directly within the context of questions of language and personal identity, the presence of the imagery of clothing should also be emphasized here. We have seen earlier how clothes form a recurrent way of describing London life—

an instant means of establishing identity where anonymity would otherwise reign—and how closely they are related to the image of the theater. (If we find it hard to imagine a society where noblemen customarily wore ribbons and glittering stars upon their chests, or where vividly colored suits, laces, and jewelry bespangled every city crowd, we have only to think of equally vivid equivalents in our own time: the haute couture of Paris, the fashionable plumage that parades down New York avenues, the gaudy équipages of Los Angeles. The theatricality that helps to define urban life is always slipping from the playhouse into the streets.) In Wordsworth's account of the Blind Beggar, the phrase "upon his chest/Wearing a written paper" resonates with a dozen other instances of clothing imagery in book VII, constituting a minor pattern that recalls both the theater and, delicately, the image of the body. His first imaginings of the city include "mitred Prelates, Lords in ermine clad" (108) and statues "addressed" in "gleaming mail" and gorgeous gowns (139–40). The theaters he frequents are part masquerade; the "comely bachelor" in the pulpit preaches "Fresh from a toilette of two hours" (552). Finally, he cuts short his task of describing London's vices:

> Folly, vice,
> Extravagance in gesture, mien, and dress,
> And all the strife of singularity,
> Lies to the ear, and lies to every sense—
> Of these, and of the living shapes they wear,
> There is no end.

[VII, 578–83]

The episode of the Blind Beggar follows closely upon this dismissal, but the label he wears differs in every way from such frivolous, mimicking lies or even from the label of the invisible actor ("Bold delusion!"). These are deceitful, unnatural disguises; in contrast, the language of the beggar's label addresses utmost questions, it offers to say "whence he came, and who he was." The content of his story may be unutterable, but it is worn like a living star. And our inability to say what the label says is only like our inability to say what resemblance is intended in the Westminster Bridge sonnet, where

> This City now doth, like a garment, wear
> The beauty of the morning.
>
> [*PW,* III, 38]

The motif of language helps to shape Wordsworth's vision of London in other conspicuous ways. Sketches of two orators, Pitt and Burke, for example, and a satire against an exquisitely fashionable young preacher recall the distinctions we saw in the *Dunciad* between the true and false language of the city. They remind us, too, of how far Wordsworth's expectant choir of redbreasts at the beginning of book VII has been replaced by politics, blasphemy, and noise. But the encounter with the Blind Beggar points toward one further aspect of language and the city that remains to be considered. The beggar's label is written, voiceless. Wordsworth turns from it to a series of London scenes less abrupt or sublime, which nonetheless take full "Possession of the faculties":

> the peace
> That comes with night; the deep solemnity
> Of nature's intermediate hours of rest,
> When the great tide of human life stands still;
> The business of the day to come, unborn,
> Of that gone by, locked up, as in the grave;
> The blended calmness of the heavens and earth,
> Moonlight and stars, and empty streets, and sounds
> Unfrequent as in deserts; at late hours
> Of winter evenings, when unwholesome rains
> Are falling hard, with people yet astir,
> The feeble salutation from the voice
> Of some unhappy woman, now and then
> Heard as we pass, when no one looks about,
> Nothing is listened to.
>
> [VII, 654-68]

These lines, says Herbert Lindenberger, look forward to the

symbolism of the city in post-Romantic literature: "the fog of Dickens' London and the searing summer heat of Dostoevsky's Saint Petersburg, . . . the infernal cities invoked by Baudelaire, Thomson, and the early Eliot."[19] Their eerie, discomposing quality—of stillness, darkness, and unfrequent sounds—also points us backward in the poem. They recreate that mysterious alienation which Wordsworth (like De Quincey) suffered before he saw the beggar, they remind us of the blasphemous prostitute, they recall the *Trivia*-like list of sights in a tour through the city. And yet the things the poet evokes here are not unrelated to each other. This mood of the city in its "hours of rest" invites comparison with the city as Wordsworth saw it from Westminster Bridge: with the "business of the day to come" likewise "unborn," the same prospect blending "heaven and earth," the same suggestion of somehow ominous quiet, "as in the grave." London is as deserted now at midnight as at dawn. Only the "feeble salutation" of "some unhappy woman"—no curse—is sometimes heard, but not listened to. As in the Westminster Bridge sonnet, the city is full of silences. Once more we may be tempted to regard this silence as unurban, the city most unlike itself, for all along one of the distinguishing characteristics of London has been its ceaseless speech: from the street cries celebrated in the *Spectator,* to Pope's collapsing language, to Johnson's clubs; even Defoe's doomed city echoes with the mournful cry, "Bring out your dead." But the indistinct voice of the prostitute sounds to us like the unconnected, uncommunicating voices of the streets that modern literature takes as the city's truth, and prepares us for the cacophony of Bartholomew Fair to come. Ultimately it moves us beyond both city and natural world toward the inarticulated world of the poet's transcendent, autonomous imagination. Caught in this moment is what G. Wilson Knight finds in the late poem called "The Power of Sound": "the art deepest in Wordsworth—the invisible, the haunting and mysterious art of music; or, rather, just of sound, the sob and surge of eternal seas, the ultimate language of the depths of being; sound which is all but silence."[20]

V

One of the commonest ways to describe eighteenth-century London—or any great city, of course—has been to stress the movement of its crowds: the flux of motion on its streets, the hurry and bustle of its traffic. But two ways of making this energy coherent are commonly used. The first is to give the movement itself a metaphoric unity—a "stream" of people, the "full tide" of human existence—so that its undifferentiated nature is formed into a shape. (Even so extreme a presentation as Swift's inundated London in "A Description of a City Shower" is unified at least by the metaphor of flood; Steele varies the formula when he organizes the city's movement according to "The Hours of London.") The disorder of the streets can also be shaped in a second way, by placing a steadfast symbolic building in opposition to the fluidity of the crowd: St. Paul's Cathedral serves this function in any number of travel books and especially in pictures and engravings, where it rises majestically above the common rush (in an indirect fashion so too does Pope's Whitehall in *Windsor-Forest*).[21] And both ways are sometimes used at once, as in the recurrent picture of the Stock Exchange in London, a building that *contains flux,* an architectural discors concordia.

But here is Bartholomew Fair, Wordsworth's culminating image for the city in *The Prelude.*

> What a shock
> For eyes and ears! what anarchy and din,
> Barbarian and infernal,—a phantasma,
> Monstrous in colour, motion, shape, sight, sound!
> Below, the open space, through every nook
> Of the wide area, twinkles, is alive
> With heads; the midway region, and above,
> Is thronged with staring pictures and huge scrolls,
> Dumb proclamations of the Prodigies;
> With chattering monkeys dangling from their poles,
> And children whirling in their roundabouts;
> With those that stretch the neck and strain the eyes,
> And crack the voice in rivalship, the crowd

> Inviting; with buffoons against buffoons
> Grimacing, writhing, screaming,—him who grinds
> The hurdy-gurdy, at the fiddle weaves,
> Rattles the salt-box, thumps the kettle-drum,
> And him who at the trumpet puffs his cheeks,
> The silver-collared Negro with his timbrel,
> Equestrians, tumblers, women, girls, and boys,
> Blue-breeched, pink-vested, with high-towering plumes.
> All moveables of wonder, from all parts,
> Are here—Albinos, painted Indians, Dwarfs,
> The Horse of knowledge, and the learned Pig,
> The Stone-eater, the man that swallows fire,
> Giants, Ventriloquists, the Invisible Girl,
> The Bust that speaks and moves its goggling eyes,
> The Wax-work, Clock-work, all the marvellous craft
> Of modern Merlins, Wild Beasts, Puppet-shows,
> All out-o'-the way, far-fetched, perverted things,
> All freaks of nature, all Promethean thoughts
> Of man, his dullness, madness, and their feats
> All jumbled up together, to compose
> A Parliament of Monsters. Tents and Booths
> Meanwhile, as if the whole were one vast mill,
> Are vomiting, receiving on all sides,
> Men, Women, three-years Children, Babes in arms.
>
>   Oh, blank confusion! true epitome
> Of what the mighty City is herself. . . .
>   [VII, 685–723]

Discordia discors: no attempt is made to organize this chaos. The only metaphors the poet offers are of perverted order ("A Parliament of Monsters," a "vast mill . . . vomiting"). The only continuity is in his tone of outrage. No relationship with landscape connects us with the larger world, as in the Westminster Bridge sonnet or *Windsor-Forest.* The fair comes upon Wordsworth like an avalanche of sensation, and his immediate response is to escape it, distancing himself as he always does from overpowering spectacles.[22] Awkwardly he implores the Muse to lift him above the crowd—in contrast to the kind of self-distancing he earlier achieves by trance or daydream in the busy streets—but the invocation is as inadequate as awkward, and he slips back helplessly into "anarchy and din,/Barbarian and infernal." The phrase recalls Milton's description of Hell as "a universe of Death" and therefore the earlier allusion in book VII to London and Hell (81–82). But the allusion falls away like flotsam as Wordsworth rushes into a random, jarring list of images and items without form, an ugly list that imitates the chaotic effect it describes. In his revulsion from the Midway's procession, indeed, he seems to parody his own pleasure in London's sights; and lines 694–703, which follow so closely upon the beautiful passage describing the silent city, emphatically shatter that mood of solemn lyricism with their tumbling, unorchestrated sounds of kettle-drums, trumpets, hurdy-gurdies, and cracked voices: the city of language has disintegrated into "staring pictures and huge scrolls,/Dumb proclamations" of the fair's exhibits, and the "rivalship" of "buffoons" like Dunces "Grimacing, writhing, screaming." And then the motif of clothing reappears in the gaudy crowd "Blue-breeched, pink-vested, with high-towering plumes," and with it the city's body, monstrous and vomiting.

We must go back to Pope for anything like Wordsworth's anger in the presence of this prototypical London disorder, and even then we are likely to feel that Wordsworth's response erupts along more elemental lines, that his personality is more vulnerable to such a shock and more deeply violated. To earlier observers like John Strype the fair was immoral enough: "of little other Use, than for idle Youth, and loose People to resort to," consisting chiefly of "Debaucheries, Drunkenness, Whoredom, and in seeing and hearing Things not fit for Christian Eyes and Ears."[23] (Moll Flanders begins an assignation there.) Even Ned Ward finds its uproar disconcerting. Yet Wordsworth draws back, so it seems, in actual fright. Some sources of fear he names: lost identity, lost distance, "Oppression, under which even highest minds/Must labour" (VII, 729–30), unmanageable energy. But we may also surmise that the relentless *human* character of the fair disturbs him and strains his resolution not to give way to a solipsistic imagination, separate from natural forms. As early as the second edition of *Lyrical Ballads* (1801), he had observed that

> a multitude of causes, unknown to former times, are now acting with a combined force to blunt the discriminating power of the mind, and, unfitting it for all voluntary exertion, to reduce it to a state of almost savage torpor. The most effective of these causes are the great national events which are daily taking place, and the increasing accumulation of men in cities, where the uniformity of their occupations produces a craving for extraordinary incident. . . .[24]

This craving of city dwellers for stimulation is one reason, as Hartman notes, that "so much space is given in Book VII to fairs and festivals, to primitive and sophisticated amusement, in a word, to distractions. Their existence shows the imaginative impulse asserting itself blindly, yet being reduced to superstition and torpor by too quick or crude a satisfaction."[25] Wordsworth describes the torpor of Bartholomew Fair by a metaphor frequent in his poetry: it "lays,/If any spectacle on earth can do,/The whole creative powers of man asleep!" (VII, 679–81). But this festive sleep differs entirely from those trancelike visionary moments that the poet sometimes enters: what in the Immortality Ode he calls the "fields of sleep." The sleep of London brings neither glory nor dream to him. Instead, the restless movement of the crowds "All jumbled up together" suggests a related but negative idea of sleep, the stirrings of the mind at a level just below consciousness, the anarchic riot of the unconscious when it is unsteadied by any principle of control.

Pope's Bartholomew Fair represented the decline of artistic standards in Augustan London: the reader was invited to measure the Smithfield theater and its rabble audience against the achievement of earlier cities. Wordsworth balances Bartholomew Fair, not against an earlier and more elevated standard, but against the modest "rustic fair" on Mount

Helvellyn with which book VIII begins. In contrast to the
infernal din of London, the language of this festival is clear,
intelligible. He asks rhetorically:

> WHAT sounds are those, Helvellyn, that are heard
> Up to thy summit, through the depth of air
> Ascending, as if distance had the power
> To make the sounds more audible?
>
> [VIII, 1–4]

What seems a crowd to the "solitary hill" is in fact "but a
little family of men,/Shepherds and tillers of the ground"
(VIII, 7–8), an organized gathering of men with wives and
children, not the confusion of "Men, Women, three-years
Children, Babes in arms." As we follow Wordsworth's loving
description of this fair, moving like a camera across it, we
may be struck with the realization that in his London there
had been no order because there had been no repetition: no
sacred place was repeated, as in Eliade's theory; no great city
in the past; and in the long catalogue of sights in Bartholomew Fair nothing recurred, nothing fixed in a pattern. The
"blank confusion" of the city was a consequence of its unending temporality. But on Helvellyn the poet takes care to
stress the ritual nature of the fair. It is a seasonal festival,
"repeated," one that Helvellyn "Sees annually." Those who
come are familiar faces, like the speechmaker or the aged
woman who "finds her way again,/Year after year, a punc-
tual visitant!" (VIII, 30–31). Children play contentedly
among the livestock and the scattered stalls as an "ancient
wedded pair" engages in the repetition of memory. They

> Sit in the shade together, while they gaze,
> "A cheerful smile unbends the wrinkled brow,
> The days departed start again to life,
> And all the scenes of childhood reappear."
>
> [VIII, 47–50]

Finally, the movement of this small crowd appears unhurried,
calm; no metaphor of stream or tide shapes their energy;

their stir is animating and protected, loved. They play like children, watched over by an ordering and nurturing Nature:

> They move about upon the soft green turf:
> How little they, they and their doings, seem,
> And all that they can further or obstruct!
> Through utter weakness pitiably dear,
> As tender infants are: and yet how great!
> For all things serve them: them the morning light
> Loves, as it glistens on the silent rocks;
> And them the silent rocks, which now from high
> Look down upon them; the reposing clouds;
> The wild brooks prattling from invisible haunts;
> And old Helvellyn, conscious of the stir
> Which animates this day their calm abode.
>
> [VIII, 58–69]

Helvellyn presents a counterexample to London's chaos; in the passage immediately beforehand, the passage following Bartholomew Fair and with which book VII closes, Wordsworth essays an explanation of its source of order. The "perpetual whirl" of the city is "By nature an unmanageable sight," except to "him who looks / In steadiness," Wordsworth says, thinking of himself:

> who hath among least things
> An under-sense of greatest; sees the parts
> As parts, but with a feeling of the whole.
>
> [VII, 733–36]

And to the question of how such "under-sense" is gained, he replies that it springs from early knowledge of natural forms, in their ordering repetition, above all in their "everlasting" changelessness. He names the enduring forms that save him from the trivial sleep of the city and all its "self-destroying, transitory things":

> Think, how the everlasting streams and woods,
> Stretched and still stretching far and wide, exalt
> The roving Indian, on his desert sands:
> What grandeur not unfelt, what pregnant show

Of beauty, meets the sun-burnt Arab's eye:
And, as the sea propels, from zone to zone,
Its currents; magnifies its shoals of life
Beyond all compass; spreads, and sends aloft
Armies of clouds,—even so, its powers and aspects
Shape for mankind, by principles as fixed,
The views and aspirations of the soul
To majesty.

[VII, 745–56]

Colin Clarke has observed two concepts that run continually through Wordsworth's poetry and that we may feel to be at work here and in the preceding lines. First is the sense of penetration, which takes the poet through the surfaces of things toward their "under-sense"; and closely related is the act of looking "In steadiness" that such penetration requires. In book IV Wordsworth tells how festivals and parties in the summer—distractions that sound like a milder and miniature Bartholomew Fair—had led to "an inner falling off" like that experienced in London. His deeper vision is described in an elaborate simile of vision and commingled objects:

   As one who hangs down-bending from the side
Of a slow-moving boat, upon the breast
Of a still water, solacing himself
With such discoveries as his eye can make
Beneath him in the bottom of the deep,
Sees many beauteous sights—weeds, fishes, flowers,
Grots, pebbles, roots of trees, and fancies more,
Yet often is perplexed, and cannot part
The shadow from the substance. . . .

[IV, 256–64]

And on this Clarke remarks, "The quest for reality, or real things, is both a movement in depth and a sustained endeavour to part the solid from the illusory."[26] Reality, illusion: Wordsworth's London has been an unreal city from the beginning, fit for epic, a moving surface that reflects but not discloses, an opaque, resistant stream where the condition of true vision is transparency. *The Prelude* is not about failure, as the

Dunciad is, but it is in part about the failure of the city. The illusion of theater in London has been the illusion it gives of life; for a time the poet has grown reconciled to unrealities. Now the long swell of anger that rolls across book VII subsides in the stern, unanswerable sermon on "forms/Perennial" that rise above the city and against it: mountains, sea, desert, and "everlasting streams and woods."

Postscript:
"In Londons opening Streets"

Immediately the Lark mounted with a loud trill from
  Felphams Vale
And the Wild Thyme from Wimbletons green &
  impurpled Hills
And Los & Enitharmon rose over the Hills of Surrey
Their clouds roll over London with a south wind,
  soft Oothoon
Pants in the Vales of Lambeth weeping oer her Human
  Harvest
Los listens to the Cry of the Poor Man: his Cloud
Over London in volume terrific, low bended in anger.

This is William Blake at the conclusion of his long prophetic
poem *Milton* (42:29–35).[1] If we search for a similar voice
in the eighteenth century—a similar way of weaving passions,
metaphor, and detail—we will sooner or later come to think
of Pope. A city of anger, a city of salvation, improbable
lyric beauty created out of the names of places and people,
surrealistic giant forms, above all a systematic context, inherited or self-forged, which shapes poetry in a fallen world,
much as a forest may enclose a meadow: in their common
images and themes Blake is a poet such as Pope might have
become, had the times chosen.

I

Blake was born in London in 1757. The date is often over-
looked, for we tend to class him with a later generation of

Romantic poets and to neglect his inevitable affinities with the midcentury world, the age of Johnson, in which he was reared. But the affinities are clear and firm and unmistakable.

> I wander thro' each charter'd street,
> Near where the charter'd Thames does flow.
> And mark in every face I meet
> Marks of weakness, marks of woe.
>
> In every cry of every Man,
> In every Infants cry of fear,
> In every voice: in every ban,
> The mind-forg'd manacles I hear
>
> How the Chimney-sweepers cry
> Every blackning Church appalls,
> And the hapless Soldiers sigh,
> Runs in blood down Palace walls
>
> But most thro' midnight streets I hear
> How the youthful Harlots curse
> Blasts the new-born Infants tear
> And blights with plagues the Marriage hearse.

Blake's "London" is the legitimate inheritor of the Augustan tradition exemplified by *Trivia,* the vision of the walker in the city who records and organizes London. His London too is a city of sounds—the mournful wails that punctuate each step, the appalling sighs and curses—and we may for a moment be reminded of Defoe's weeping London or of Pope's insanely noisy Dunces; but Blake's voices are addressed to no one, these are not the street cries that so charmed Addison and Gay, and no one besides the poet listens. The cries indeed have become curses by the poem's end, linked in our minds perhaps to the Billingsgate present everywhere in the *Dunciad* and linked, even more directly, to that moment in *The Prelude* when Wordsworth, walking the midnight streets, hears the feeble call of "some unhappy woman." But the differences in Blake's version are powerful and instructive. The harlot's curse, neither chaotic nor corrupt language in Pope's sense, lacks the bawdy vitality of Mother Needham; we feel no tug of kinship and sympathy as Wordsworth does when he thinks of the woman's unhappiness, a kind of shared alienation. Blake's narrow streets echo with desperate repetitions (cry, mark, charter'd, ev'ry); his scene rings with voices—but not with words—an insubstantial city, an unbodied chorus of lamentation. Raymond Williams speaks of the poem as establishing a new way of seeing London in English literature, a new way of pointing up the connections between the city's misery and the systematic exploitation of the poor by capitalism.[2] If we pause to visualize it, however, the effect is bizarre, dreamlike, phantasmagoric: we see, not connections, but disjunctions, not system, but disintegration.

The connections Williams has in mind are apparent in the implicit political judgments of the poem's diction. The "charter'd" streets and river—"dirty" in Blake's first draft— suggest the official licenses of commercial London, the language of privilege, and they mock, as David Erdman observes, the "charter of the land" of freedom in James Thomson's "Rule, Britannia!"[3] Chimney sweepers and prostitutes are casually expendable commodities in an economy that crushes and demeans, while "hapless Soldiers" may refer to the troops disbanded after the American Revolution (and hence unemployed) or to the mutinous soldiers of the stormy years 1793–94; even the "blackning Church," coated with factory soot, has a social as well as metaphorical truth. But the political and economic background constitutes the least important part of the poem for readers in any age—we are far more likely to respond to the permanent images of a city that we encounter in almost every line: to the image of language, for example, or to the presence of the river once again. The dirty Thames that flows through Blake's London, for all its grim ambiguities of charter, has a common source with that crystal artery of commerce Defoe and so many others celebrate, and with those still older rivers that stream across the classical world from Troy.

The harlot and the newborn infant remind us indirectly that great cities can be symbolized as mothers, as in Pope's Dulness with her brood and Wordsworth's prostitute and lovely boy: their civilizing walls enclose a cradle. Indeed, in the first three stanzas of the poem one senses an absence of fathers in the world of the city—a fearful withdrawal of masculine authority—and in the last stanza, climaxing the devastation of London, one senses an absence of virtuous mothers. Blake's harlot, moreover, not only evokes the image of perverted motherhood—made yet more poignant by her youth—but also associates it with the blinding venereal disease passed on from mother to child: this London is built up of faces, tears, and blood, like a body. And if our minds go back to Defoe's plagued London for comparison, we may see too that Blake's city is doomed—"blasted"—for its sins and that this plague like Defoe's is no extraordinary event, but simply the condition of London as it always is, a prison of the spirit, a city that traffics in death, whose carriages are hearses and whose "manacles" are everywhere.

No golden spires, no temples, domes, or theaters—Blake's unholy "London" by the relentless pressure of its vision almost compels us to call forth its opposite. Instinctively at some level we resist its hopelessness. Line 3 originally read "And see in every face I meet"; the repetition of "mark" strengthens our sense of the poem as chant and of the poet's activity; but it also strengthens the allusion Blake is surely making to Ezekiel 9:4:

> And the LORD said unto him, Go through the midst of the city, through the midst of Jerusalem, and set a mark upon the foreheads of the men that sigh and that cry for all the abominations that be done in the midst thereof.

The marks that the Lord commands are signs of salvation, not destruction: those who weep shall be comforted. How far Blake intends us to take the analogy it is impossible to know, whether the city is to be saved or, as the mournful cries suggest, to be slain. In line 8 Blake first wrote "The german forg'd manacles I hear," alluding to the Hanoverian King George III, whom he had already attacked in *America* (1793). Had he left the line unaltered, it would be easier to find along with Raymond Williams that the poem discloses the tyrannical political and economic connections of early industrial capitalism: the foreign king, the *imposition* of chains point toward an outside force that oppresses the poor, the helpless, the weak. But Blake's inspired substitution of "mind" for "german" removes completely this sense of otherness; the manacles, as Williams himself recognizes, are "imposed and yet self-imposed"; the blood on palace walls can be the soldiers' own. "London" may urge us with unprecedented irony to revolution against this terrifying city, may attack its most sacred institutions of palace, church, and marriage—but these institutions are self-affrighting artifacts. Despite the power of his indictment, Blake conveys no indication that London is an external force beyond our power to order and control, as it is for Defoe, Pope, and Wordsworth. No poet is more sensitive than Blake to the presence of "contraries" in human life, to the necessity for more than one way of seeing a thing. The *Songs of Innocence* do not offer a counterpart to the London of *Experience;* but the very systems that seem to hold the city in lonely bondage can vanish in a moment. "I must Create a System, or be enslav'd by another Mans," cries Los in *Jerusalem;* "I will not Reason & Compare: my business is to Create" (10:20–21). What is new in Blake's great poem is not political and economic insight—that can be found in other forms in other works—it is that Blake has transformed London into a state of mind as well as an actual city, a symbol into which we seem to have entered and from which we can return. If Babylon can be built by human imagination in self-betrayal, cannot in mind-forged freedom Jerusalem be built?

II

The image of the city appears surprisingly late in Blake's poetry.[4] A passing description of London in the dramatic fragment "King Edward III" (1782) satirizes the mode of praise into which Pope and Thomson sometimes fall and gives one further turn to the trope of the hive:

> . . . while my father
> Toils in his wars, and turns his eyes on this
> His native shore, and sees commerce fly round
> With his white wings, and sees his golden London,

And her silver Thames, throng'd with shining spires
And corded ships; her merchants buzzing round
Like summer bees, and all the golden cities
In his land, overflowing with honey. . . .

[ii, 7–14]

Otherwise, apart from "London" itself in *Songs of Experience*
(1794) and scattered references elsewhere, the image of a city
moves to the center of Blake's thought only in Night V of his
incohesive epic *The Nights of the Four Zoas* (1803?), where
the prophetic figure Los is first seen building the holy city
Golgonooza. The lateness of this appearance surprises us in
part because the insistently pastoral character of many of
Blake's early lyrics, particularly in *Songs of Innocence* (1789),
almost requires a demonic city like "London" to act as foil;
an implicit criticism of city life rises irresistibly in our minds
as we proceed from the introduction of "Innocence" through
"The Shepherd," "The Echoing Green" and on to "The
Chimney Sweeper" and "Holy Thursday," poems which can
only be construed as profoundly antiurban. And indeed,
when Blake and his wife set out on their ill-fated removal to
Felpham in Surrey in September 1800, the criticism becomes
briefly explicit; their correspondence for several months flares
with comparisons between "the terrible desart of London,"
as Catherine Blake calls it, and the countryside: "Felpham
is a sweet place for Study," Blake writes John Flaxman on
September 21, "because it is more Spiritual than London.
Heaven opens here on all sides her Golden Gates; her windows
are not obstructed by vapours; voices of Celestial inhabitants
are more distinctly heard, & their forms more distinctly seen,
& my Cottage is also a Shadow of their houses."[5] But Blake's
growing disbelief in the "otherness" of natural objects—his
emerging conviction that human imagination itself, not an
external God, creates the world that it inhabits—leads him
necessarily toward a conception of the imagination as continually *building,* and thence to the greatest of all symbols
of human building, the city.

Blake's own imagination generally proceeds by formulating
oppositions, "contraries," and placing them in conflict (often

called inaccurately a dialectical procedure); the structure of his thought is invariably a simple one, although its elaborations grow complex beyond the patience of all but academic readers. The Golgonooza that Los begins to construct in *The Four Zoas* appears to stand midway between the unhumanized London of Experience, the "real" London that Defoe or Boswell might have charted, and the holy city of Jerusalem. But in truth Golgonooza and London together represent positive and negative human life in the fallen world, a world distinguished from the eternal world of Jerusalem by its enslavement to time and to a nature not yet fully malleable to imagination. Jerusalem and her shadow Babylon exist beyond time and space as apocalyptic cities. Or as Thomas R. Frosch concisely notes, "Golgonooza is to Jerusalem as Spenser's Cleopolis is to his New Jerusalem. It contains the best of this world, and it is a haven; but just as there is a distinction between art and life, so Golgonooza is art within nature. The city Jerusalem, on the other hand, replaces the world of pain, and in Eden the distinction of art and life vanishes."[6] We may think of these city-states as Blake found them in Revelation, perpetually at war until the victory of the New Jerusalem; or, given Blake's resonant capacity for irony, we may think of them as parodies of each other, distortions of imagination loosely comparable to satire. But from our point of view it is more profitable to see them as humanized and unhumanized cities: those like Golgonooza which are projected out of the living human imagination and those like "London" which wrongly submit to the fallen belief in a nonhuman natural world. In *The Four Zoas,* Los begins to build Golgonooza out of a fear of "Eternal Death & Uttermost Extinction" (60:2), simply as a place of retreat from sorrow; once discovered, however, the symbolism of warring cities first dominates and then organizes the drama of Blake's prophecies.

As in all epics, the action of *Jerusalem* (1804–18?) advances toward a city. It is the restoration of Jerusalem, "a City yet a Woman" (F.Z. IX: 122:18), to Albion, fallen eternal man, for which the prophet Los labors ceaselessly in the poem, a "labor" so stressed and lamented that comparison with Virgil and the *labor* of founding Rome must occur to many readers. And as in the *Aeneid,* the final city is reached only by passing through and destroying lesser ones. The lowliest, the first to be transcended is the unhumanized "London" of Experience, which Blake now describes by blending topography and dogma in the service of his own arcane mythology. Like Diogenes with his lantern, for example, in chapter 2 Los enters the interior of Albion's bosom carrying a globe of fire with which to search out the enemies of the eternal man. In vain, however, he passes among the rocks and caves of death.

> He came down from Highgate thro Hackney & Holloway
>   towards London
> Till he came to old Stratford & thence to Stepney &
>   the Isle
> Of Leuthas Dogs, thence thro the narrows of the Rivers
>   side
> And saw every minute particular, the jewels of Albion,
>   running down
> The kennels of the streets & lanes as if they were abhorrd.
> Every Universal Form, was become barren mountains
>   of Moral
> Virtue: and every Minute Particular hardend into grains
>   of sand:
> And all the tendernesses of the soul cast forth as filth
>   & mire,
> Among the winding places of deep contemplation intricate
> To where the Tower of London frownd dreadful over
>   Jerusalem:
> A building of Luvah builded in Jerusalems eastern gate
>   to be
> His secluded Court: thence to Bethlehem where was
>   builded
> Dens of despair in the house of bread: enquiring in vain
> Of stones and rocks he took his way, for human form
>   was none.
>
>   [45:14–27]

As Los moves from north to south along the eastern edge of London, toward the river, the language winds deliberately between familiar place-names like Highgate and Stepney and recondite names like Leutha and Luvah, at once recalling familiar images of the city and compressing them into a system of meaning. The "Isle/Of Leuthas Dogs" thus refers to the Isle of Dogs in the dockyards of the Thames, site of the East India Company wharves and notorious for prostitutes, and also Blake's female character Leutha, who represents sexuality as it is conventionally associated with sin and guilt; the conjunction of sexual and imperial commerce symbolizes—and explains—to Blake one aspect of London's despair.[7] Again, the great river is followed in this passage by its polluted parodies, the kennels that sweep the city's jewels (its poor) through the streets "as if they were abhorrd"; the "filth & mire" the kennels carry are not the debris that Swift and Gay observed, but the "Minute Particulars" that form one tenet of Blake's revolt against neoclassicism and by which he means individual men and women rather than categories or classes. The artifacts he goes on to name brood ominously over a repressive Gothic London—the Tower, a secluded Court, the lunatic asylum of Bethlehem (which means in Hebrew "house of bread")—and we feel ourselves trapped in its silent "winding places . . . intricate," still lost in a "charter'd" city. Appropriately for such a city of death, the imagery is predominantly mineral; in its hard towers and dungeons no human forms appear. Yet we notice that curiously these structures belong to Jerusalem as well as London (lines 23–24). This abrupt intrusion of Jerusalem could momentarily suggest the "contrary" of London, the standard against which it is measured, just as Pope's constant evocation of Rome in the *Dunciad* suggests the contrary of Dultown; but whereas Pope's intention is to mock one city with another, Blake's syntactical fantasia creates instead an impression of continuity, of interchangeability. London is to *become* Jerusalem in Blake's apocalypse, as one state of mind gives way to a higher. "The Cities & Villages of Albion became Rock & Sand Unhumanized," the poet cries (63:18), but rock, sand, and all barren, inhuman forms will yield like shadows when the sunlight comes.

III

"The City of Golgonooza. . . is the spiritual fourfold London, in the loins of Albion" (*M* 20:39–40). The first chapter of *Jerusalem* contains the most elaborate of Blake's descriptions of Golgonooza, a comprehensive survey of the city Los and his workers build in the fallen world with "terrible eternal labour" while they await the awakening of Albion. The description begins in Blake's own questioning voice:

> What are those golden builders doing? where was the
>   burying-place
> Of soft Ethinthus? near Tyburns fatal Tree? is that
> Mild Zions hills most ancient promontory; near mournful
> Ever weeping Paddington? is that Calvary and Golgotha?
> Becoming a building of pity and compassion? Lo!
> The stones are pity, and the bricks, well wrought
>   affections:
> Enameld with love & kindness, & the tiles engraven gold
> Labour of merciful hands: the beams & rafters are
>   forgiveness:
> The mortar & cement of the work, tears of honesty:
>   the nails,
> And the screws & iron braces, are well wrought
>   blandishments,
> And well contrived words, firm fixing, never forgotten,
> Always comforting the remembrance: the floors, humility,
> The cielings, devotion: the hearths, thanksgiving:
> Prepare the furniture O Lambeth in thy pitying looms!
> The curtains, woven tears & sighs, wrought into lovely
>   forms.
>   [12:25–39]

Once again, familiar names from London geography serve to anchor Blake's verse beneath overlayings of Christian and mythological allusion: "Tyburns fatal Tree" is Tyburn gallows, for centuries London's place of public execution,

located north of Hyde Park along the present-day Edgeware
Road; "mournful/Ever weeping Paddington" was a slum dis-
trict being rapidly rebuilt around 1811–14 (it may be
"weeping" because of the abundant natural springs there);
Lambeth is the section of Southwark where Blake's inspira-
tion first came to him.[8] "Ethinthus," buried near Tyburn
and Zion, is a character from *The Four Zoas;* Golgotha, it
has been suggested, forms the root of Golgonooza. Harold
Bloom likens the entire passage to George Herbert's poem
"The Church Floor"—a striking comparison, reminding us of
Blake's deep allegorical temper (despite his own denial).[9]
Herbert's *The Temple,* moreover, of which "The Church
Floor" is one part, identifies worship and salvation with
church building—a commonplace throughout Christian Europe in the Renaissance—and Herbert literally imitates the
process in his book, from the door of the temple with which
he begins to the Eucharistic altar with which he concludes.
Blake's Golgonooza forms a considerably less sanguine
allegory. The articles of building are made to stand for pious
affections like forgiveness and humility, but the city is pitted
everywhere with places of death—Calvary, Golgotha, Tyburn's
tree—and the effect is one of suffering and sadness more than
thanksgiving. A humanized city undeniably, Golgonooza still
exacts its terrible penitential labor; and in the last lines of the
introduction, Blake reminds us why this should be so:

> Go on, builders in hope: tho Jerusalem wanders far away,
> Without the gate of Los: among the dark Satanic wheels.
> [12:43–44]

The long, comprehensive account of Golgonooza that follows these lines is based largely upon Ezekiel. Assuming the
"fourfold" vision of the prophet, Blake proceeds around the
four walls of the city, which are also points of the compass,
describing them in terms of the human body, wheels, minerals,
animals, and gates.

> And the Four Points are thus beheld in Great Eternity
> West, the Circumference: South, the Zenith: North
> The Nadir: East, the Center, unapproachable for ever.

These are the four Faces towards the Four Worlds of
    Humanity
In every Man. Ezekiel saw them by Chebars flood.
And the Eyes are the South, and the Nostrils are the East.
And the Tongue is the West, and the Ear is the North.
And the North Gate of Golgonooza toward Generation;
Has four sculpturd Bulls terrible before the Gate of iron.
And iron, the Bulls: and that which looks toward Ulro,
Clay bak'd & enamel'd, eternal glowing as four furnaces:
Turning upon the Wheels of Albions sons with enormous
    power.
And that toward Beulah four, gold, silver, brass & iron.
                                            [12:54–66]

Each gate is treated this way in turn, and the interior of the
city is briefly imaged by Blake's symbols of womanhood,
Luban, which is the vagina, and the golden Looms of Cathedron. Outside the protective walls, as Eliade might have pre-
dicted, surrounding Golgonooza "lies the land of death eternal;
a Land/Of pain and misery and despair and ever brooding
melancholy," a terifying world "Incoherent" where human
imagination has not yet cast its light (13:30–55). In this
world Albion sleeps.

Against Golgonooza and its shadow London, Blake places
the eternal city Jerusalem and her shadow Babylon. Chapter 1
of the prophecy, which opens with Albion gripped by the
sleep of death, closes with his long, moving lament over what
he has lost.

O Jerusalem Jerusalem I have forsaken thy Courts
Thy Pillars of ivory & gold: thy Curtains of silk & fine
Linen: thy Pavements of precious stones: thy Walls of pearl
And gold, thy Gates of Thanksgiving thy Windows of
    Praise:
Thy Clouds of Blessing; thy Cherubims of Tender-mercy
Stretching their Wings sublime over the Little-ones of
    Albion.
O Human Imagination O Divine Body I have Crucified

I have turned my back upon thee into the Wastes of Moral
    Law.
                                                    [24:17-24]

This has been seen by Bloom as a derivation from Ezekiel,
but is more fundamentally derived from Revelation, not
Ezekiel, for while a prophetic book suits a city forever to
be built (ever weeping, always comforting), an apocalyptic
book is necessary for the eternal one.[10] Blake first shows us,
to borrow categories from Northrop Frye, the process of his
building, and then the product. Jerusalem is resplendent with
golden pillars, walls of pearl, pavements of jewels, triumphantly more glorious than the homely bricks and tiles of
Golgonooza. And the place of woman in Blake's city has
radically altered. We no longer see the Looms of Cathedron
weaving, but the precious curtains and linen woven; we no
longer see a city of iron walls and barricaded gates, but the
beautiful body of a bride like that in Revelation, divine,
maternal, whose cherubims stretch "their Wings sublime over
the Little-ones of Albion." These glories, however, Albion
has rejected, choosing the antithetical city Babylon, whose
walls

. . . are Souls of Men: Her Gates the Groans
Of Nations: her Towers are the Miseries of once happy
    Families.
Her Streets are paved with Destruction, her Houses built
    with Death
Her Palaces with Hell & the Grave; her Synagogues with
    Torments
Of ever-hardening Despair squard & polished with cruel
    skill.
                                                    [24:31-35]

The stones and towers of Babylon are like those of fallen
London when Los enters it; only the human forms in tor-
ment, the groans and souls of nations, establish it as the
universal Hell into which any man may fall, if he chooses
materialism, rationalism, convention over the realities of

imagination. Elsewhere Blake portrays Babylon as Vala, the scarlet woman to whom Albion turns in his error.

The condition of Albion, as *Jerusalem* makes plain, will not always be fallen. Nor has he always been bound in labyrinthine delusion, caught in the nets of Vala. Once Babylon

> . . . wast lovely as the summer cloud upon my hills
> When Jerusalem was thy hearts desire in times of youth
> & love.
> Thy Sons came to Jerusalem with gifts, she sent them
> away
> With blessings on their hands & on their feet, blessings of
> gold,
> And pearl & diamond: thy Daughters sang in her Courts:
> They came up to Jerusalem; they walked before Albion
> In the Exchanges of London every Nation walkd
> And London walkd in every Nation mutual in love &
> harmony
> Albion coverd the whole Earth, England encompassed the
> Nations,
> Mutual each within others bosom in Visions of
> Regeneration;
> Jerusalem coverd the Atlantic Mountains & the Erythrean,
> From bright Japan & China to Hesperia France & England.
> [24:36–47]

The existence of a golden age is necessary, of course, to the myth of a fall; but the astonishing image of the Exchanges of London as places "mutual in love & harmony" carries us suddenly back toward the prosperous urbanity of Addison and Defoe, and the vision of England encompassing the nations in spiritual empire carries us back toward the empire Pope saw radiating outward from Windsor Forest. Nowhere, perhaps, than in *Jerusalem* are Blake's links with Augustan literature more visible and extensive. If we set it beside the greatest epic of the neoclassical age, the *Dunciad* of 1743, we discover a continuity that goes far to reclaim Blake for the eighteenth century. The *Dunciad,* for example, shows England falling into sopor ("Say how the Goddess bade Britannia

sleep,/And pour'd her Spirit o'er the land and deep" [I, 7–8])
and universal darkness. *Jerusalem*—a mighty maze, but not
without a plan—shows Albion-England awakening into eternal
light:

> Of the Sleep of Ulro! and of the passage through
> Eternal Death! and of the awaking to Eternal Life. . . .
> Awake! awake O sleeper of the land of shadows, wake!
>   expand!
>
>   [4:1–6]

Both poems center about the symbol of a City of Art, one
that Pope inherits from antiquity and one that Blake forges
for himself; and both poems depict the fallen cities of the
present as versions of contemporary London, populated with
the poets' personal enemies (like Blake's Scofield and Pope's
Colley Cibber) and constructed from actual names of London
streets and places—all meaningless to modern readers without
a critical apparatus of forbidding proportions. Then too, each
poem, epic and mock-epic, tells the story of the restoration
of the goddess of the city; and Dulness and Jerusalem, in the
great tradition of urban symbolism, are both mothers, and
each encloses a mighty river. (Even tributaries of the Thames
like Fleet Ditch and Tyburn's Brook are counterpointed in
their poetic geography.) Above all, beyond coincidences of
imagery and form, both Pope and Blake look out upon a
world broken into fragments, a world gone mad with too
much or too little reason, a world whose disorder cries out
for reintegration of all its warring, resistant parts.

Pope chose to heal by satire, Blake by prophecy. Their
similarities ought not be unduly stressed. When we come to
Blake's London after Defoe's, Pope's, Johnson's and Wordsworth's, the distance between the humanistic and the visionary
imaginations looms as impressively as ever. In the humanistic
imagination, the city possesses an objective, absolute reality
of its own—Defoe's London is quantitative, statistical, beyond
human scale in its size and power; Pope's London is a dark
image of that real city of beauty in which he believes and
which is ordained by powers outside ourselves; Wordsworth's

ideal London resembles that community of natural forms
with which he continually converses. In every case, their
sense of reality is from without, and their metaphors for
London are invocations of the more than human. But Blake
finds in London "mind-forg'd" forms, expressly human, not
beyond the human; self-creations, not divine creations. Perhaps indeed he has the better right to be called "humanist,"
since the city he sees is the city he has built, projected from
his own regenerated vision. But custom has decreed that the
term be given to those minds which are inclined, like Johnson's, to accept the reality of stubborn stones, cities of other
people, and the limits of a shared imagination.

IV

Blake is not alone in his power to see an unearthly city.
Toward the end of book II of *The Excursion,* composed
during the summer of 1806, Wordsworth yielded momentarily to his own visionary impulse and set forth another
version of the New Jerusalem. The narrator of the poem, at
this point called the Solitary, has joined a rescue party in the
northern mountains, searching for an old man caught over-
night by a violent storm. As they return with him, the Solitary falls behind the others.

> . . . a step,
> A single step, that freed me from the skirts
> Of the blind vapour, opened to my view
> Glory beyond all glory ever seen
> By waking sense or by the dreaming soul!
> The appearance, instantaneously disclosed,
> Was of a mighty city—boldly say
> A wilderness of building, sinking far
> And self-withdrawn into a boundless depth,
> Far sinking into splendour—without end!
> Fabric it seemed of diamond and of gold,
> With alabaster domes, and silver spires,
> And blazing terrace upon terrace, high
> Uplifted; here, serene pavilions bright
> In avenues disposed; there, towers begirt

    With battlements that on their restless fronts
    Bore stars—illumination of all gems!
                [PW, V, 71–72; bk. II, 829–45]

Like Blake's great city, this too is drawn from Revelation:
it descends from heaven, it blazes into sight, it has no need
of sun or moon to lighten it. Wordsworth's "wilderness of
building," however, seems to us more remote than Blake's
somehow. It is not personified like Jerusalem, a city yet a
woman; he does not enter it or speak; it remains at a distance
atop the mountains—an "unimaginable sight"—independent
and anonymous.

    Clouds, mists, streams, watery rocks and emerald turf,
    Clouds of all tincture, rocks and sapphire sky,
    Confused, commingled, mutually inflamed,
    Molten together, and composing thus,
    Each lost in each, that marvellous array
    Of temple, palace, citadel, and huge
    Fantastic pomp of structure without name,
    In fleecy folds voluminous, enwrapped.
                                [II, 853–60]

It has neither architecture nor structure, only a strange ar-
resting force too unambiguous to be typically Wordsworthian.
The moment is prophetic, the Solitary says, one "Such as by
Hebrew Prophets were beheld/In vision—forms uncouth of
mightiest power/For admiration and mysterious awe" (II,
867–69). Yet he responds to its glory with a melancholy
prayer for self-annihilation:

                    . . . my heart
    Swelled in my breast—"I have been dead," I cried,
    "And now I live! Oh! wherefore *do* I live?"
    And with that pang I prayed to be no more!
                                [II, 874–77]

After a time, although the apparition had not faded, he
"descended."
    The old man who had been rescued from these mountains
died a few days later, peacefully, of no obvious physical

cause. Geoffrey Hartman points out how the Solitary's vision on the mountain and subsequent descent seem to mirror the old man's night in the storm, spent in a ruined chapel, and his death: everything hints "at death by vision as well as water."[11] Everything hints likewise at the incompatibility of imagination and natural life. The Solitary sees "the revealed abode/Of Spirits in beatitude," a city so gloriously absorbing that the valley beneath him, "a dwelling-place of Man," for a time becomes invisible and, afterward, intolerable in comparison. He dreams of a city like Yeats's Byzantium, where he can be gathered "into the artifice of eternity." Our impulse is to recall other "spots of time" in which imagination lunges forward suddenly to capture Wordsworth's consciousness, but the Solitary's vision resists this company. The city, inorganic, remote, permits no tension between the ordinary world of process and its own molten forms; the Solitary gazes enraptured, but moves at last, not toward it, but toward the world of cottages, hearths, and death below. Its otherness is absolute.

Two years later, in April 1808, after an extended stay in London, Wordsworth wrote from Grasmere to his friend Sir George Beaumont in faint puzzlement. His relations with Coleridge during the visit had been difficult and anxious; his dealings with his publisher and other friends had also been uneasy. "You will deem it strange," he wrote to Sir George, "but really some of the imagery of London has, since my return hither, been more present to my mind than that of this noble vale."[12] Then followed a careful description of the snowy morning on which he began his journey from the city, walking past Temple Bar, up Fleet Street, along Ludgate Hill toward St. Paul's; and in a notebook passage of blank verse, never published by the poet, he described the same memorable occasion once again. Let this be one last artifact of urbanity, to stand against the Solitary's vision:

> PRESS'D with conflicting thoughts of love and fear
> I parted from thee, Friend, and took my way
> Through the great City, pacing with an eye

Downcast, ear sleeping, and feet masterless
That were sufficient guide unto themselves,
And step by step went pensively. Now, mark!
Not how my trouble was entirely hush'd,
(That might not be) but how, by sudden gift,
Gift of Imagination's holy power,
My Soul in her uneasiness received
An anchor of stability.—It chanced
That while I thus was pacing, I raised up
My heavy eyes and instantly beheld,
Saw at a glance in that familiar spot
A visionary scene—a length of street
Laid open in its morning quietness,
Deep, hollow, unobstructed, vacant, smooth,
And white with winter's purest white, as fair,
As fresh and spotless as he ever sheds
On field or mountain. Moving Form was none
Save here and there a shadowy Passenger
Slow, shadowy, silent, dusky, and beyond
And high above this winding length of street,
This moveless and unpeopled avenue,
Pure, silent, solemn, beautiful, was seen
The huge majestic Temple of St. Paul
In awful sequestration, through a veil,
Through its own sacred veil of falling snow.

[*PW*, IV, 374–75]

All this we have seen before in Wordsworth and in other writers of London. He leaves the city as he left it in 1802, on the morning of the Westminster Bridge sonnet, surprised by its power to move him, drawn toward a silent, unpeopled scene in which London is least like itself and most like nature, "Laid open in its morning quietness" almost unto the fields and to the sky. Here too is the recurrent landmark of the city's strength, St. Paul's; the image of clothing in the veil of snow; the meditations of the walker in the city. The litany of "Ships, towers, domes, theatres, and temples" is reproduced in "Deep, hollow, unobstructed, vacant, smooth." The circumstances also remind us of Wordsworth's ascent of Mount Snowdon in *The Prelude,* when he looked up to see the moon, clouds, and a hundred hills with "dusky backs"; and of his recollection of crossing the Alps, when Imagination rose from his mind's abyss; and of his trancelike progress through the London crowds, lost in thought, until the face of the Blind Beggar admonished him. No one would rank this spot of time with those, of course: the conflict that distracts the poet remains vague; the verse is in places flaccid, propped by unnecessary repetition and lines of adjectives. An easy poem to parody. The whole experience belongs to the category Hartman names "the halted traveller," like the Solitary's dream in *The Excursion,* in which consciousness of self expands toward a heightened consciousness of imagination's separate reality and toward thoughts of death. Yet Wordsworth here does not penetrate into the meaning of his symbol, though he looks upon it steadily; nor does the image of St. Paul's lead him to thoughts of death—instead it comforts him, like an "anchor of stability." Such comfort is all the more welcome in the deep, hollow alienation of the moment, when other passengers move slowly like shadows, unreachable and unalive, and snow blankets the city like a shroud. We may feel for an instant the coming loneliness of later writers of the city in the nineteenth and twentieth centuries; in the snow we may discern the first intimations of a unifying device, like the brown fog of Dickens and Eliot, which obliterates the city's chaos, though at the cost of its energy. Perhaps only alienation like this makes possible that freer imagination which Blake and so many others have come to value.

Wordsworth, however, concludes in security, gazing at "The huge majestic Temple of St. Paul." It is a sight that must also have greeted Defoe or Pope or Johnson in their time, in snow, in rain, in darkness; but none of them thought it worthwhile to record the moment as Wordsworth has. His is a new sensibility, more nearly like our own. Still, it would be hard to find a better image for all of their Londons, not only because for three centuries the church has served as virtual synecdoche for the city, but also because a temple is traditionally a place, like a mountain, where the heavens and the earth are joined. Solitary, troubled by questions of friendship and self, Wordsworth is anchored like all of us to the great city in which he walks; but as he looks upward he also sees the image of a holy city, purer, more beautiful than this one, yet bound to it inseparably in his imagination.

Notes

Introduction

1 James Boswell, *London Journal, 1762–1763,* ed. Frederick A. Pottle (New York: McGraw-Hill, 1950), pp. 43–44. The quotation from Christopher Morley appears in his preface to this volume, p. xxix. From the same site Wordsworth, in his "Extempore Effusion upon the Death of James Hogg," more somberly reflects:

> Our haughty life is crowned with darkness,
> Like London with its own black wreath,
> On which with thee, O Crabbe! forth-looking,
> I gazed from Hampstead's breezy heath.

(*Poetical Works,* ed. Ernest de Selincourt and Helen Darbishire, 5 vols. [Oxford: Oxford University Press, 1940–49], IV, 277.)

2 V. S. Pritchett and Evelyn Hofer, *London Perceived* (London: Chatto and Windus, Heinemann, 1962). Dunbar is quoted from *Chronicles of London,* ed. C. L. Kingsford (Oxford: Oxford University Press, 1905), p. 253.

3 Paul Fussell, *The Rhetorical World of Augustan Humanism* (Oxford: Oxford University Press, 1965).

4 Leonard Barkan, *Nature's Work of Art: The Human Body as Image of the World* (New Haven: Yale University Press, 1975).

5 Sigmund Freud, *Civilization and Its Discontents,* trans. James Strachey (New York: W. W. Norton and Co., 1962), p. 17.

6 Laurence Sterne, *Tristram Shandy,* ed. Ian Watt (Boston: Houghton Mifflin, 1965), p. 35.

7 Edward Ward, *The London Spy,* I, ii, 5 (London, 1698). See also James Sutherland, "John Gay," in *Pope and His Contemporaries: Essays Presented to George Sherburn,* ed. James L. Clifford and Louis A. Landa (New York: Oxford University Press, 1949), pp. 201–14, and Sutherland, *Background for Queen Anne* (London: Methuen, 1939), a delightful collection of essays on English social history.

8 Geoffrey Scott, *The Architecture of Humanism: A Study in the History of Taste,* 2nd ed. (New York: Charles Scribner's Sons, 1969), p. 174.

Chapter One

1 *A Tour thro' the Whole Island of Great Britain,* ed. G. D. H. Cole, 2 vols. (London: Peter Davies, 1927). All further quotations are from this edition.

2 *A Journal of the Plague Year,* ed. Louis A. Landa, Oxford English Novels (London: Oxford University Press, 1969). All further quotations are from this edition.

The stress upon London as a marketplace is widely felt in the earlier part of the century. James Thomson's account of London in "Autumn," for example, moves from a celebration of its order and its role as "Nurse of art" to trade, focusing like Defoe's upon the river:

> Then commerce brought into the public walk
> The busy merchant; the big warehouse built;
> Raised the strong crane; choked up the loaded street
> With foreign plenty; and thy stream, O Thames,
> Large, gentle, deep, majestic, king of floods!

(*Complete Poetical Works,* ed. J. Logie Robertson [London: Oxford University Press, 1908], p. 137, ll. 118–22.) Cf. John Dyer, *The Fleece* (1757), II. ll. 626–30, and also Richard Glover, *London; or, The Progress of Commerce* (1739), passim.

3 *Moll Flanders,* ed. George A. Starr, Oxford English Novels (London: Oxford University Press, 1971). All further quotations are from this edition.

4 Succeeding quotations from the *Tour* are from I, 316–18. Here and in the rest of this chapter I am in strong disagreement with Raymond Williams, who in *The Country and the City* (New York: Oxford University Press, 1973), pp. 145–46, suggests that London's "monstrosity" becomes an important image only late in the eighteenth century.

Defoe like most observers points out that London's extraordinary growth "has been generally made in our time, not only within our memory, but even within a few years" (*Tour,* I, 295). Horace Walpole compares London ironically to Rome and speculates about its ultimate size: "As its present progress is chiefly north, and Southwark marches south the metropolis promises to be as broad as long. Rows of houses shoot out every way like a polypus; and so great is the rage of building everywhere, that if I stay here a fortnight, without going to town, I look about to see if no new house is built since I went last." (To Sir Horace Mann, 16 July 1776. *Correspondence,* ed. W. S. Lewis [New Haven: Yale University Press, 1937–], 24:228.)

5 *The Tricks of the Town Laid Open,* in *The Tricks of the Town,* ed.
Ralph Straus (London: Chapman and Hall, 1927), p. 11. The examples given in my text could be multiplied indefinitely. J. Stuart,
for example, confronts the image directly when he speaks against
those who find London already overgrown in *Critical Observations
on the Buildings and Improvements of London* (London, 1771),
p. 41:

> The argument on this topic commonly urged with the greatest
> triumph is, "That a large head is a certain indication of a weak and
> distempered body." Granting even the premises to be true . . . ,
> this is still concluding from metaphor; a species of reasoning fit
> to be employed with like success on either side. For example,
> one might with equal justice assert London to be the heart, which
> the more capacious it is found, and the freer the circulation
> through it, the more life and strength it imparts; and ingenious
> men might hit upon other allusions to parts of the human body,
> whose size commonly denotes vigour and health.

Defoe, in fact, does compare London to an overgrown liver in *The
Complete English Tradesman* (London, 1727), II, ii, 129. Cf. Tom
Brown, *Amusements Serious and Comical, Calculated for the Merid-
ian of London* (London, 1702), p. 42, and also Anon., *A Satirical
View of London at the Commencement of the Nineteenth Century*
(London, 1801), p. 4. Leonard Barkan's recent study, cited above,
intro., n. 4, treats the whole subject in rich detail. A curious miscel-
lany of other figures for London is found in Edward Hatton, *A New
View of London* (London, 1708), I, i. See also the thorough essay
by Louis A. Landa, "London Observed: The Progress of a Simile,"
PQ, 54 (Winter 1975): 275–88, which came to hand after the present chapter was completed.
6 Josiah Tucker, *Four Letters . . . to the Earl of Shelburne,* 2nd ed.
(London, 1783), pp. 44–45. A striking difference between Cobbett's *Rural Rides* (1830) and Defoe's *Tour,* incidentally, is the extent to which London dominates the earlier work, organizing and
harmonizing every aspect of English life, while it figures in the later
book only as a point of contrast with the still-healthy English countryside.
7 Defoe, *The Storm* (London, 1704), pp. 81–82. ("Heads" in this
quotation refers to categories in a list.) Again, in *Giving Alms No
Charity* (London, 1704), p. 18, Defoe writes that "This Breach of
the Circulation of Trade [in London] must necessarily Distemper

the Body. . . ." Images of disease, thwarted trade, and London frequently occur together in his writing.

8 *The Complete English Tradesman,* I, xiii.

9 Anon., written in 1578, included in the appendix to John Strype's edition of John Stow's *Survey of London* as "A Discourse of London . . ." (London, 1747), II, 2.

10 John Milton, *Complete Poetry and Major Prose,* ed. Merritt Y. Hughes (New York: Odyssey Press, 1957), pp. 744–45.

11 See Mark Schorer's introduction to the Modern Library edition of *Moll Flanders* (New York: Random House, 1950), and the chapters on Defoe in Ian Watt's *The Rise of the Novel* (Berkeley and Los Angeles: University of California Press, 1957).

12 *The Complete English Tradesman,* II, ii, 142.

13 *Giving Alms No Charity,* p. 5.

14 See, for example, the preface to *The Complete English Tradesman,* I, vi.

15 Benjamin Boyce, "The Question of Emotion in Defoe," *Studies in Philology,* 50 (1953):45–58 partially reprinted in my *Defoe: A Collection of Critical Essays* (Englewood Cliffs, N.J.: Prentice-Hall, 1975). For another perspective see the brilliant essay by Leo Braudy, "Daniel Defoe and the Anxieties of Autobiography," *Genre,* 6 (1973):76–97.

16 Anon., *The Country Spy; or, A Ramble thro' London* (London, n.d.), p. 1.

17 Voltaire, *Lettres anglaises,* ed. Fernand Massé (Utrecht: Jean-Jacque Pauvert, 1964), Sixième lettre, p. 44. Addison's description may be found in *Spectator* No. 69, 19 May 1711. Cf. Fielding's ironic comments in "An Essay on the Knowledge of the Characters of Men," *Miscellanies,* ed. Henry Knight Miller (Oxford: Oxford University Press, 1972), I, 177. Ned Ward's description follows that of Bedlam and stresses confusion and variety; he also uses a familiar image: "An Incessant Buz, like the Murmurs of the distant Ocean, stood as a *Diapason,* to our talk, like a *Drone* to a Bagpipe" (*The London Spy,* I, iii, 13–15).

18 *The Complete English Tradesman,* II, ii, 108. The fullest discussion of this question is Hans H. Andersen, "The Paradox of Trade and Morality in Defoe," *Modern Philology,* 39 (1941):23–46.

19 Defoe, *The True and Genuine Accounts of the Life and Actions of the Late Jonathan Wild* (London, 1725), p. 28.

20 Quoted in Paul Zweig, *The Adventurer* (New York: Basic Books, 1974), p. 104.

21 Defoe, *Augusta Triumphans; or, The Way to Make London the Most Flourishing City in the Universe* (London, 1728), p. 48. Cf. part I of Defoe's much earlier *Reformation of Manners* (London, 1702). The most elaborate discussion of the connection between London's trade and its luxury and vice occurs in the final two chapters of *The Complete English Tradesman.*

22 Defoe, *Some Considerations on . . . Seamen* (London, 1728), p. 44. These same urchins are described with Dickensian charm, of course, in the early pages of *Colonel Jack.*

23 Defoe, *Due Preparations for the Plague, as Well for Soul as Body,* ed. George A. Aitken (London: J. M. Dent, 1895), p. 28.

24 Anon., *Hell upon Earth,* p. 1. Previous quotations are from the title page.

25 I rely on M. Dorothy George's masterful *London Life in the Eighteenth Century* (London: Kegan Paul, 1925; rpt. New York: Harper and Row, 1964), pp. 24–27. A more recent discussion will be found in George Rudé, *Hanoverian London 1714–1808* (Berkeley and Los Angeles: University of California Press, 1971), pp. 4–10.

26 Fielding, *An Enquiry into the Causes of the Late Increase of Robbers* (London, 1751), p. 76. (In 1723, however, the privilege of sanctuary was removed from the Mint.) W. H. Auden calls the image of city as desert an emphatically Romantic motif, but it appears not infrequently in early eighteenth-century literature. See *The Enchaféd Flood* (New York: Random House, 1950), p. 36.

27 Ben Sedgly, *Observations on Mr. Fielding's Enquiry* (London, 1751), pp. 22–23.

28 Bernard Mandeville, *An Essay on Charity Schools,* in *The Fable of the Bees,* ed. F. B. Kaye (Oxford: Oxford University Press, 1924), I, 272. Cf. his remarks on London's size, I, 306.

29 *The Fable of the Bees,* I, 11–12.

30 *The Adventurer,* chap. 8. I am indebted throughout this section to Zweig's fine book.

31 Steen Rasmussen, *London, the Unique City,* rev. ed. (London: Jonathan Cape, 1948), p. 23.

32 *Serious Reflections of Robinson Crusoe,* in *Works,* ed. G. H. Maynadier (Boston: D. Nickerson, 1903–04), II, 6.

33 *The Adventurer,* pp. 144–45.

34 Anon., *The Cheats of London Exposed* (London, 1766), p. 83. Another anonymous pamphlet, *Critical Remarks on Sir Charles Grandison, Clarissa, and Pamela* (London, 1754), p. 54, echoes this charge and links it to London's prosperity: "Neither can such char-

acters as Lovelace and his associates, or mother Sinclair and her nymphs, display themselves, or such a place as the mother's brothel, subsist any where but in a city like London, the overgrown metropolis of a powerful Empire, and an extensive commerce."

35 *The Country and the City,* p. 227. The extent of the complexity is illustrated by this notice from the *Weekly Journal,* 30 March 1717, quoted in James P. Malcolm, *Anecdotes of the Manners and Customs of London during the Eighteenth Century* (London, 1810), I, 104–05: "The Thieves have got such a villainous way now of robbing gentlemen, that they cut holes through the back of Hackney-coaches, and take away their wigs, or fine head-dresses of gentlewomen; so a gentleman was served last Sunday in Tolley-street, and another but last Tuesday in Fenchurch-street; wherefore, this may serve for a caution to gentlemen or gentlewomen that ride single in the night-time, to sit on the fore-seat, which will prevent that way of robbing."

To George A. Starr I owe the observation that one other group indirectly "ratifies" the labyrinthine city: those writers like Defoe in his *Tour,* Gay, Dunton, Ward in their very different tours, who seem to master London's confusion by mapping it.

36 Tobias Smollett, *Peregrine Pickle,* ed. James L. Clifford, Oxford English Novels (London: Oxford University Press, 1964), p. 679. W. B. Carnochan approaches this theme from another point of view in *Confinement and Flight: An Essay on English Literature of the Eighteenth Century* (Berkeley and Los Angeles: University of California Press, 1977), as does my essay, "The Madhouse, the Whorehouse, and the Convent," *Partisan Review,* Summer 1977.

37 W. Austin Flanders, "Defoe's *Journal of the Plague Year* and the Modern Urban Experience," *Centennial Review,* 16 (1972):328–48; reprinted in my *Defoe: A Collection of Critical Essays.*

38 See Jacques Ellul, *The Meaning of the City,* trans. Dennis Pardee (Grand Rapids, Mich.: William B. Eerdmans Publishing Co., 1970), especially chap. 1. On the question of magic see Robert E. Park, "Magic, Mentality, and City Life," in *The City,* ed. Robert E. Park, Ernest W. Burgess, and R. D. McKenzie (Chicago: University of Chicago Press, 1967).

39 William Blake, *A Vision of the Last Judgment,* in *The Poetry and Prose of William Blake,* ed. David V. Erdman, commentary by Harold Bloom (Garden City, N.Y.: Doubleday, 1970), p. 555.

40 See n. 5 to chap. 2 below. Landa and others have found a geographical patterning to the movement of the plague—see his extensive notes in the edition cited—but the ordinary reader would not, I think, perceive a design.

41 *Due Preparations for the Plague,* p. 102.
42 William Wordsworth, *Poetical Works,* ed. Ernest de Selincourt and Helen Darbishire, 5 vols. (Oxford: Oxford University Press, 1940–49), II, 217.
43 Pope to Hugh Bethel, 9 Aug. 1726, in *Correspondence,* ed. George Sherburn (Oxford: Oxford University Press, 1956), II, 387. Cf. Gay's letter to Pope: "I find myself in such a strange confusion and Depression of Spirits, that I have not Strength even to make my Will; though I perceive by many warnings, I have no continuing City here" (III, 20). Gay alludes to Hebrews 13:14: "For here we have no continuing city, but we seek one to come."

Chapter Two

1 Unless otherwise noted all quotations of Pope's poetry are from his *Poetical Works,* ed. Herbert Davis (London: Oxford University Press, 1966). Reference is frequently made to the Twickenham Edition of Pope's *Poems,* ed. John Butt et al. (London: Methuen, 1938–67). For a discussion of the relationship between Pope's description of Eden and Milton's see Sanford Budick, *Poetry of Civilization: Mythopoeic Displacement in the Verse of Milton, Dryden, Pope, and Johnson* (New Haven: Yale University Press, 1974), pp. 120–24.
2 Maynard Mack, *The Garden and the City: Retirement and Politics in the Later Poetry of Pope, 1731–43* (Toronto: University of Toronto Press, 1969), p. 3. The name Augusta was given by the Romans to a number of colonial towns, including London, during and after the reign of Augustus.
3 "On Reading Pope," *College English,* 7 (1945–46):263–73.
4 Evelyn Waugh, *Helena* (London: Chapman and Hall, 1950), p. 47. Quoted in Alvin B. Kernan, *The Plot of Satire* (New Haven: Yale University Press, 1965), p. 142.
5 Mircea Eliade, *Cosmos and History: The Myth of the Eternal Return,* trans. Willard Trask (New York: Harper, 1959), pp. 10–18. One reason for the impression of chaos and monstrosity that London makes upon eighteenth-century writers, besides its size, is perhaps the fact that it lacks a defining boundary to mark it off as a place of order. The ancient walls of the City, though still standing then, were for the most part obscured by unplanned new building; along the north side the city shaded gradually into the countryside. See also Sigmund Freud, *Civilization and Its Discontents,* p. 40.
6 Lewis Thomas, *The Lives of a Cell* (New York: Viking Press, 1974), p. 12.

7 In *The Seasons,* James Thomson also uses the beehive to describe the city: "Autumn," ll. 105–08, and "Winter," ll. 631–32 (*Poetical Works,* ed. J. Logie Robertson). The image enters Western literature, of course, through Virgil, from *Georgics,* IV, 149–281, and *Aeneid,* I, 430–36. In *The Image of the City and Other Essays,* ed. Anne Ridler (Oxford: Oxford University Press, 1958), Charles Williams cites Canterbury's speech in *Henry V,* I, ii, as a major Renaissance instance. Other important examples in our period are found in Abraham Cowley's "The Wish," John Dryden's *Annus Mirabilis* (verse 28), and John Denham's *Coopers Hill.* See also the bees and their "Straw-built Citadel" in *Paradise Lost,* I, 768 ff.

8 See especially chap. 6 of Mack, *The Garden and the City.*

9 Pope, *Correspondence,* ed. George Sherburn (Oxford: Oxford University Press, 1956), II, 330. See Louis Bredvold's influential essay "The Gloom of the Tory Satirists," conveniently reprinted in *Eighteenth-Century Literature,* ed. James L. Clifford (New York: Oxford University Press, 1959).

10 Aubrey Williams, *Pope's Dunciad: A Study of Its Meaning* (Baton Rouge: University of Louisiana Press, 1955), especially chaps. 1 and 2.

11 The best modern guide to the physical appearance of the city throughout the period is John Summerson, *Georgian London,* rev. ed. (London: Barrie and Jenkins, 1970). See also chap. 1 of Pat Rogers, *Grub Street: Studies in a Subculture* (London: Methuen, 1972), and chap. 2 of George, *London Life in the Eighteenth Century.* An unsurpassed account of the topography of central and western London at midcentury is Hugh Phillips, *Mid-Georgian London* (London: Collins, 1964). A good collection of contemporary impressions is *London in Flames, London in Glory,* ed. R. A. Aubin (New Brunswick, N.J.: Rutgers University Press, 1943). See also the *Covent-Garden Journal,* no. 37 (1752).

   The "ample bow" that Pope observes in *Windsor-Forest* has been seen ingeniously by Earl R. Wasserman as "also the bent bow of Heraclitus which illustrated for him the harmony of oppositions" (*The Subtler Language* [Baltimore: Johns Hopkins University Press, 1959], p. 167). The Twickenham notes to the poem give two other instances of the same figure, in Charles Hopkins's *White-Hall* and Abraham Cowley's *On the Queen's Repairing Somerset House.*

12 Emrys Jones is quoted from "Pope and Dulness," in *Pope: A Collection of Critical Essays,* ed. J. V. Guerinot (Englewood Cliffs, N.J.: Prentice-Hall, 1972), p. 146.

   In the first version of the *Dunciad* Pope seized upon a perfect symbol for the battle. By 1728 many of the churches built under Anne's decree in 1711 were literally collapsing because of poor construction and materials. Others served mainly impious appetites: the church of St. Mary-le-Strand near Temple Bar had replaced an ancient maypole in 1718—an undeniably pagan emblem—but soon attracted prostitutes (saints) instead of worshipers.

> Where the tall May-pole once o'erlook'd the *Strand;*
> But now (so ANNE and Piety ordain)
> A Church collects the saints of *Drury-lane.*
>
> [II, 11–13]

13 Jones, pp. 147–51. All succeeding quotations are from the 1743 *Dunciad.*

14 Quotations from Pope's Homeric translations are taken from the Twickenham volumes, ed. Maynard Mack (London: Methuen, 1967). The importance of Proteus as a destroyer of cities is discussed in A. Bartlett Giamatti, "Proteus Unbound: Some Versions of the Sea God in the Renaissance," in *The Disciplines of Criticism,* ed. Peter Demetz, Thomas Greene, and Lowry Nelson, Jr. (New Haven: Yale University Press, 1968).

15 Quoted in George, p. 85. Other accounts may be found in Rogers, pp. 142–60, and in John Ashton, *The Fleet: Its Rivers, Prisons, and Marriages* (London, 1888). An early satiric description is Ben Jonson's poem "The Famous Voyage," in *Works,* ed. C. H. Herford and Percy and Evelyn Simpson (Oxford: Oxford University Press, 1947), VIII, 84–89.

16 *The Works of Edmund Spenser: A Variorum Edition,* ed. Edwin Greenlaw, Charles G. Osgood, and Frederick M. Padelford (Baltimore: Johns Hopkins University Press, 1932–57), III, 135.

17 Jung's view is set forth in C. G. Jung, *Symbols of Transformation,* trans. R. F. C. Hull (Princeton: Princeton University Press, 1956), pp. 207 ff. Lewis Mumford in *The City in History* (New York: Harcourt Brace Jovanovich, 1961), pp. 12–13, argues that "Woman's presence made itself felt in every part of the village: not least in its physical structures, with their protective enclosures, whose further symbolic meaning psychoanalysis has now tardily brought to light. Security, receptivity, enclosure, nurture—these functions belong to woman; and they take structural expression . . . in the house and the oven, the byre and the bin . . . and from there pass on to the city, in the wall and the moat, and all inner spaces, from the atrium to the cloister. House and village, eventually the town itself, are woman writ large. . . . In Egyptian hieroglyphics 'house' or 'town'

may stand as symbols for 'mother'. . . ." An anonymous pamphlet, *London: A Satire* (London, 1780), p. 2, complains in the same vein: "THIS town contains an assemblage of houses, which are called in the aggregate—the Metropolis; *i.e.* the Mother City." And yet the femininity of the city, Paul Grinestier writes, may also be traced to "the ancient myth of the terrible and sterile woman Medeusa, one of the three Gorgons . . . [whose] eyes had the power of transforming anyone who beheld her to stone. . . . In this way the modern city continues the line of all the heroines who suffer Diana's complex—sanguinary cruelty toward Acteon—that of the woman who, instead of being a mother, is a destroyer: Delilah, Helen, Lucretia Borgia, the Arlesienne, etc." (*The Poet and the Machine,* trans. Martin B. Friedman, [Chapel Hill: University of North Carolina Press, 1961], pp. 57–58).

For reasons of her own Mrs. Shandy insists on lying-in in London.

18 See Traugott Lawler, "'Wafting Vapours from the Land of Dreams': Virgil's Fourth and Sixth Eclogues and the *Dunciad,*" *Studies in English Literature* (Summer 1974), pp. 373–86.

19 Further discussion of this point may be found in Michael V. De Porte, *Nightmares and Hobby-Horses: Swift, Sterne, and Augustan Ideas of Madness* (San Marino: Huntington Library, 1974), and in chap. 3 of my own *Visits to Bedlam: Madness and Literature in the Eighteenth Century* (Columbia: University of South Carolina Press, 1974).

20 The OED cites three instances from Blackmore's poem: III, 266; VI, 464; VII, 632. Pope used the word in the original *Dunciad* in another context: "And pin'd, unconscious of his rising fate" (I, 110). The word appears several times in his Homeric translations. See Emmet G. Bedford and Robert J. Dilligan, *A Concordance to the Poems of Alexander Pope* (Detroit: Gale, 1974),and also n. 21, below.

21 Sigmund Freud, *Civilization and Its Discontents,* p. 40. Characteristic references to the Cloaca Maxima may be found in Juvenal, V, 105; Livy, I, 56, 2; the elder Seneca, *Controversiae,* 3, praef. 16. In a related image, Oliver Goldsmith compares London to "a vast munificent dunghill," (*Works,* ed. Arthur Friedman [London: Oxford University Press, 1966], II, 280). Other representative instances of this motif applied to the presence of foreigners are in *Tricks of the Town,* p. 190: "LONDON is the grand Reservoir, or Common-Sewer of the World: Like the Ocean, wherein the muddy and dirty Brooks, as well as the clear and rapid Rivers, disembogue

themselves, this City receives the Scum and Filth, not only of our
own, but of all other Countries . . ."; and in William Cowper's poem
"Retirement," ll. 681–84, where the poet describes the life

in proud and gay
And gain-devoted cities. Thither flow,
As to a common and most noisome sew'r,
The dregs and feculence of ev'ry land.

(*Poems,* ed. Hugh I'Anson Fausett, Everyman's Library [London:
J. M. Dent, 1931].)

22 The OED quotes John Ray, for example, in 1714: "It is also ob-
servable that the Sinks of the Body are removed as far from the
Nose and Eyes as may be."

23 Quotations are from Swift's *Poetical Works,* ed. Herbert Davis (Oxford: Oxford University Press, 1967). The best essay on the poem
is by Brendan O Hehir, "The Meaning of Swift's 'Description of a
City Shower,'" *ELH* (1960), pp. 194–207.

24 Martin Price, *To the Palace of Wisdom* (New York: Doubleday,
1964), p. 259. The lines may actually refer to Dido and Aeneas in
their cave; see O Hehir, pp. 200 and 203.

25 Quotations are from Gay's *Poetical Works,* ed. G. C. Faber (Oxford:
Oxford University Press, 1926).

26 Many readers have seen *Trivia* as more profound than its title. For
them its subject is not London but something larger. "London is
Gay's emblem for actuality," according to one recent study, "for
Life itself." The mazes, alleys, and "smutty Dangers" (II, 36) of
the city symbolize its moral corruption, and Gay's cheerful, equable
manner is "precisely the embodiment of his meaning in this poem:
which is that, though life can be hideous, art offers us a way of
coping with it" (Martin Battestin, *The Providence of Wit: Aspects
of Form in Augustan Literature and the Arts* [Oxford: Oxford University Press, 1974], pp. 128–31). Another reader finds that "the
consciously false importance lent the material through the classical
references seems, in the long run, not entirely false after all"; for
the walker in the city joins a long parade of allegorical travelers
through life, "from Chaucer to Bunyan to Faulkner" (Patricia M.
Spacks, *John Gay* [New York: Twayne, 1965], p. 56). A severer
view also obtains. "It is not clever of Gay to ramble on for three
longish parts of a poem that gives mainly good advice on how to
walk the streets of London without getting splattered," writes
W. K. Wimsatt, who adds witheringly: "I believe his *Trivia* is a poem

much prized by historians of the city" ("The Augustan Mode in English Poetry," in *Hateful Contraries* [Lexington: University of Kentucky Press, 1965], p. 156).

27 *The Spectator,* ed. Donald F. Bond (Oxford: Oxford University Press, 1965), II, 434. All references to the *Spectator* are to this edition. Roderick Random behaves in an identical fashion in chap. 45 of Smollett's novel.

Typical descriptions of the theater may be found in chap. 7 of James Peller Malcolm's *Anecdotes of the Manners and Customs of London during the Eighteenth Century.* Hogarth's etched print "The Laughing Audience" (the subscription ticket for *The Rake's Progress*) offers a memorable picture of the London theater audience, especially of its social hierarchy and amorous disposition. A splendid account of two riots at the theater is given by Pierre Grosely, *A Tour of London,* trans. Thomas Nugent (London, 1772), I, 50–55. See Horace Walpole's letter to Sir Horace Mann, 26 November 1744, for another riot. See also the opening lines of Addison's poem "The Playhouse" and *The Connoisseur,* XLII (1754).

28 *Tricks of the Town,* p. 14.

29 Pope, *Imitations of Horace,* ep. II, 330–31. See also Mandeville, *Fable of the Bees,* "Remark M." For a modern view, see Noel P. Crist and L. A. Halbert, *Urban Sociology* (New York: Thomas Crowell Co., 1933), pp. 284 ff.

30 Rousseau's complex view of Paris is summarized in his *Confessions,* trans. J. M. Cohen (Harmondsworth: Penguin Books, 1953), pp. 155–70.

31 Giamatti, pp. 470–71. On masquerades, see Henry Fielding's early poem *The Masquerade* (London, 1738); "On the Masquerades" by Christopher Pitt in his *Poems* (London, 1727); and anon., *A Seasonable Apology for Mr. H-g-r* (London, 1724). There are also interesting descriptions in Malcolm, chap. 7. Thomas Dekker compares the theater to the Royal Exchange in *Gull's Hornbook* in *Thomas Dekker,* ed. E. D. Pendry (Cambridge: Harvard University Press, 1968), p. 98. *The Connoisseur,* LXVI (1755), proposes a naked masquerade!

32 Williams, *Pope's Dunciad,* p. 94. Pope's interest in theater is discussed in Malcolm Goldstein, *Pope and the Augustan Stage* (Stanford: Stanford University Press, 1958).

33 *Pope's Dunciad,* p. 97.

34 I quote from the convenient anthology of Pope's *Selected Poetry*

and Prose, ed. W. K. Wimsatt, Jr. (New York: Holt, Rinehart, 1951), p. 357.

35 "Dryden," *Lives of the Poets,* ed. G. B. Hill (Oxford: Oxford University Press, 1905), I, 469. In *The Rhetorical World of Augustan Humanism,* p. 130, Paul Fussell observes that "The architectural analogue for suggesting the nature of a poem goes back at least as far as Quintilian. It is revived in Renaissance humanist criticism and transmitted ·:o the eighteenth century without interruption." Cf. *Rambler* 168 (par. 3).

36 *Spectator* 69.

37 Quoted in John Ashton, *Social Life in the Reign of Queen Anne* (London, 1882), I, 134–35. Cf. anon., *The Laughing Philosopher* (Dublin, 1777), pp. 167–72.

38 Giamatti, p. 460. For Aristotle, see the *Selections,* ed. and trans. Philip Wheelwright (New York: Odyssey Press, 1951), xxxv–xxxvi, and W. D. Ross, *Aristotle* (New York: Meridian Books, 1959), pp. 76–77.

39 Williams, *Pope's Dunciad,* chaps. 1 and 2.

40 Pope, *Correspondence,* II, 219–20, 226–28. For the role of commerce, see Hugo M. Reichard, "Pope's Social Satire: Belles-Lettres and Business," in *Essential Articles for the Study of Alexander Pope,* rev. ed., ed. Maynard Mack (Hamden, Conn.: Archon Books, 1968).

41 Here White-hall, which had served as a harmonizing center of London's "ample bow" in *Windsor-Forest,* now represents the new wave of city vulgarity. The phrase "speaking monuments" is from Wordsworth, *The Prelude,* VIII, 172. See n. 10 to chap. 4 below.

42 Swift, *Tatler* 230, *Prose Works,* ed. Herbert Davis (Oxford: Basil Blackwell, 1939–68), II, 173–77. See also James Bramston, *The Art of Politicks, In Imitation of Horace's Art of Poetry* (London, 1729), p. 10, particularly the lines beginning "What's not destroy'd by Time's devouring Hand?/Where's *Troy,* and where's the *May-Pole* in the *Strand?*"

43 Part of Pope's objection in the *Dunciad* to profanity is that it levels and confuses social classes. Bonnell Thornton states this view concisely in *The Connoisseur,* CVIII (1756): "As there are some vices which the vulgar have presumed to copy from the great; so there are others which the great have condescended to borrow from the vulgar. Among these I cannot but set down the shocking practice of cursing and swearing: a practice, which (to say nothing at present of its impiety and profaneness) is low and indelicate, and places the

man of quality on the same level with the chairman at his door."
See also Mandeville, *Fable,* II, 59–60.

44 For cities and epic see A. Bartlett Giamatti, *Play of Double Senses: Spenser's Fairie Queen* (Englewood Cliffs, N.J.: Prentice-Hall, 1974), chap. 2.

Chapter Three

1 *Boswell on the Grand Tour: Germany and Switzerland, 1764,* ed. Frederick A. Pottle (New York: McGraw-Hill, 1953), p. 245.

2 Suggested by Pottle as Boswell's own title for Charles Johnson, *A General History of the Lives and Adventures of the Most Famous Highwaymen . . .* (London, 1734). See n. 20 below.

3 For an entertaining account of Charteris see Ronald Paulson, *Hogarth: His Life, Art, and Times* (New Haven: Yale University Press, 1971), I, 244–49.

4 Henry Fielding, *Joseph Andrews* and *Shamela,* ed. Martin Battestin (Boston: Houghton Mifflin, 1961).

5 Henry Fielding, *Tom Jones,* ed. Martin Battestin and Fredson A. Bowers (Oxford: Oxford University Press, 1974), II, 857.

6 *Covent-Garden Journal,* no. 4 (14 January 1752).

7 George Sherburn, "Fielding's *Amelia:* An Interpretation," in *Fielding: A Collection of Critical Essays,* ed. Ronald Paulson (Englewood Cliffs, N.J.: Prentice-Hall, 1962), p. 148, n. 3. The final paragraph of this essay makes a suggestive connection between Johnson's *Life of Savage* and *Amelia.* Even more morose is the view of London presented in Sarah Fielding's *Adventures of David Simple* (1744), a novel to which her brother apparently made important contribution.

8 Ronald Paulson, *Satire and the Novel in Eighteenth-Century England* (New Haven: Yale University Press, 1967), p. 161.

9 For extended discussion of the English mood after the fall of Walpole, see W. E. H. Lecky, *A History of England in the Eighteenth Century* (London: Longmans, Green, 1892), II, chap. 4.

10 Samuel Johnson, *Poems,* ed. E. L. McAdam, Jr., with George Milne (New Haven: Yale University Press, 1964), pp. 45–61. All quotations of Johnson's poetry are from this edition, vol. VI in the Yale Edition of the Works of Samuel Johnson. The later version by Edward Burnaby Greene, in *The Satires of Juvenal Paraphrastically Imitated, and Adapted to the Times* (London, 1764, 2nd ed.), is rather a panegyric on Scotland than an attack on London. Boswell mailed a copy to Sir David Dalrymple in 1763.

11 Ep. I, i. A well-known discussion of *London* is Mary Lascelles, "Johnson and Juvenal," in *New Light on Dr. Johnson,* ed. F. W. Hilles (New Haven: Yale University Press, 1959), pp. 35–55. A recent article critical of Professor Lascelles's approach is Howard D. Weinbrot, "Johnson's *London* and Juvenal's Third Satire: The Country as 'Ironic' Norm," *Modern Philology,* 73 (May 1976): no. 4, pt. 2, S56–S65.

12 James Burgh, *Britain's Remembrancer; or, The Danger Not Over* (London, 1746), pp. 40, 15–16. The American reaction is described in Bernard Bailyn, *The Ideological Origins of the American Revolution* (Cambridge: Harvard University Press, 1967), pp. 83–93. Cf. an early attack by John Dennis, *An Essay upon Publick Spirit . . .* (London, 1711), esp. p. 11.

13 Henry Fielding, *Enquiry into the Causes of the Late Increase of Robbers* (London, 1751), pp. 9–10.

14 Sir John Fielding, *An Account of the Origin and Effects of a Police* (London, 1758), pp. ix–x. A Mississippi table was a board game similar to bagatelle.

15 Tobias Smollett, *The Expedition of Humphrey Clinker,* ed. Angus Ross (Harmondsworth: Penguin Books, 1967), letters of May 20 through June 8.

16 See the important discussion in James W. Johnson, *The Formation of English Neo-Classical Thought* (Princeton: Princeton University Press, 1967), pp. 58 ff. See also my *Visits to Bedlam,* chap. 4, for further material concerning the image of the city as Bedlam.

17 Edward Gibbon, *The Decline and Fall of the Roman Empire* (New York: Modern Library, 1948), II, 148.

18 James Boswell, *Private Papers of James Boswell,* ed. Geoffrey Scott and Frederick A. Pottle (New York: privately printed, 1930), VII, 163.

19 James Boswell, *Life of Johnson,* ed. G. B. Hill, rev. L. F. Powell, 6 vols. (Oxford: Oxford University Press, 1934–50). Abbreviated in the text as B*LJ*.

20 James Boswell, *London Journal, 1762–1763,* ed. Frederick A. Pottle (New York: McGraw-Hill, 1950). Abbreviated in the text as *Jour.*

21 Sir Richard Steele, *The Town Talk,* no. 1 (1715), ed. J. Nichols (London, 1789), p. 17. For the Covent Garden petition see Ronald Paulson, *Hogarth,* I, 337.

22 Near Fleet prison clandestine marriages were often performed by drunken or defrocked clergymen in brandy shops and similar handy

public houses; these were sometimes legitimate marriages, sometimes guises for prostitution. See Lecky, II, 115–18.

23 Bertrand Bronson, "Boswell's Boswell," in *Johnson Agonistes and Other Essays* (Berkeley and Los Angeles: University of California Press, 1946; rpt. 1965), p. 64.

24 Boswell, *Boswell on the Grand Tour,* p. 304.

A remarkable union of Boswell's feelings occurs in this image of variety and sexuality: "I resolved to take London as one takes mercury; to intermit the use of it whenever I should feel it effect my brain, as one intermits the use of mercury when it affects the mouth. I was struck with agreeable wonder and admiration by contemplating the immensity of the metropolis and the multitude of objects. . . ." James Boswell, *Boswell in Extremes, 1776–1778,* ed. Charles McC. Weis and Frederick A. Pottle (New York: McGraw-Hill, 1970), p. 220. Mercury was used in the treatment of venereal disease.

25 Northrop Frye, "Towards Defining an Age of Sensibility," in *Fables of Identity* (New York: Harcourt, Brace, 1963), pp. 130–37.

26 Samuel Johnson, *Correspondence,* ed. R. W. Chapman (Oxford: Oxford University Press, 1952), I, 139.

27 Samuel Johnson, "Review of *A Free Enquiry into the Nature and Origin of Evil,*" in *Works* (London, 1825), VI, 54.

28 In the following passages I quote from Samuel Johnson, *The Life of Richard Savage,* ed. Clarence Tracy (Oxford: Oxford University Press, 1971).

29 See John Wain, *Samuel Johnson* (New York: Viking Press, 1974), chap. 7.

30 Arthur Murphy, *An Essay on the Life and Genius of Samuel Johnson, L.L.D.,* in *Johnsonian Miscellanies,* ed. G. B. Hill (Oxford: Oxford University Press, 1897; rpt. New York: Barnes and Noble, 1966). Abbreviated in the text as *JM.*

31 The phrase "candidates for renown" is taken from *Rambler* 144. All quotations from Johnson's periodical essays are taken from the volumes in the Yale Edition of the Works of Samuel Johnson: *The Idler and the Adventurer,* ed. W. J. Bate, J. M. Bullitt, and L. F. Powell (New Haven: Yale University Press, 1963), and *The Rambler,* ed. W. J. Bate and Albrecht B. Strauss (New Haven: Yale University Press, 1969).

32 Samuel Johnson, *Rasselas* in *Rasselas, Poems, and Selected Prose,* ed. Bertrand H. Bronson, 3rd ed. (San Francisco: Rinehart Press, 1971), chap. XLVI.

33 Joseph Wood Krutch, *Samuel Johnson* (New York: Harcourt, Brace, 1944), p. 57.
34 *Boswell in Extremes, 1776-1778*, p. 295.
35 See J. Hillis Miller, *The Disappearance of God* (Cambridge: Harvard University Press, 1963), pp. 5 ff.
36 Charles Lamb, Letter to William Wordsworth, 30 January 1801, in *The Letters of Charles and Mary Lamb,* ed. E. V. Lucas (New Haven: Yale University Press, 1935), I, 241.
37 Walter Jackson Bate, *The Achievement of Samuel Johnson* (New York: Oxford University Press, 1955), p. 137.
38 *Rasselas, Poems, and Selected Prose,* ed. Bronson, p. 62.
39 Bate, p. 62.

Chapter Four

1 *The Poetical Works of William Wordsworth,* ed. Ernest de Selincourt and Helen Darbishire, 5 vols. (Oxford: Oxford University Press, 1940-49). Abbreviated in the text as *PW.*
2 C. P. Moritz, *Travels in England in 1782,* quoted in A. R. Humphreys, *The Augustan World* (London: Methuen, 1954; rpt. New York: Harper and Row, 1963), p. 10. It comes as no surprise that Boswell makes an individual contribution to the genre: "At the bottom of the Haymarket I picked up a strong, jolly young damsel, and taking her under the arm I conducted her to Westminster Bridge, and then in armour complete did I engage her upon this noble edifice. The whim of doing it there with the Thames rolling below us amused me much" (*Jour.,* p. 255).
3 Thomas Bowles's "The South West Prospect of LONDON" was printed by John Bowles (1 May 1750) and recently reproduced as Greater London Council Publication 110 by the Graphics Department of the London County Council. See also Pierre Grosley's observation in *A Tour of London,* I, 22 ff.
4 Mary Moorman, *William Wordsworth: The Early Years, 1770-1803* (Oxford: Oxford University Press, 1957), p. 563.
5 I take the phrase "awed surprise" from Cleanth Brooks, *The Well-Wrought Urn* (New York: Harcourt, Brace, 1947), p. 5.
6 John Shebbeare, *Letters on the English Nation* (1756), quoted in Humphreys, p. 5.
7 David Ferry, *The Limits of Mortality: An Essay on Wordsworth's Major Poems* (Middletown, Conn.: Wesleyan University Press, 1959), p. 12. Wordsworth offered an interesting revision of the poem in a letter to John Kenyon, Autumn 1836, printed in *The*

Letters of William and Dorothy Wordsworth: The Later Years, 1821-1850, ed. Ernest de Selincourt (Oxford: Oxford University Press, 1939), II, 812.

8 Ferry, p. 14.

9 Thomas De Quincey, *Autobiography,* in *Collected Writings,* ed. David Masson (Edinburgh, 1889), I, 180-81.

10 Wordsworth, *The Prelude,* ed. Ernest de Selincourt, 2nd ed. rev. Helen Darbishire (Oxford: Oxford University Press, 1959). All quotations from *The Prelude* are taken from this edition. Unless otherwise noted, I quote from the 1850 version. In the preceding sentence in the text, I conflate phrases from the openings of books I and VII.

11 Geoffrey H. Hartman, *Wordsworth's Poetry, 1787-1814* (New Haven: Yale University Press, 1964 and 1971), p. xiii.

12 William Empson, *Some Versions of Pastoral* (New York: New Directions, 1950), p. 6.

13 *Lettre à M. d'Alembert,* in *Oeuvres complètes de J. J. Rousseau,* ed. V. D. Musset-Pathay (Paris: Chez P. Dupont, 1824), II, 120.

14 *The Works of Charles and Mary Lamb,* ed. E. V. Lucas (London: Methuen, 1903), I, 39-40.

15 J. Hillis Miller, "The Stone and the Shell: The Problem of Poetic Form in Wordsworth's Dream of the Arab," in *Mouvements premiers: Etudes critiques offertes à Georges Poulet* (Paris: Librairie José Corti, 1972), p. 130.

16 Herbert Lindenberger, *On Wordsworth's "Prelude"* (Princeton: Princeton University Press, 1963), p. 88.

17 Mandeville's essay forms part of *The Fable of the Bees*; Lamb's essay is "On the Decay of Beggars in the Metropolis," *Works,* II. A typical attack on beggars for their part in London crime is found in anon., *The Vices of the Cities of London and Westminster* (Dublin, 1751), p. 18. "Just heaven!" declares Yorick in Sterne's *Sentimental Journey,* "for what reasons hast thou order'd it, that beggary and urbanity, which are at such variance in other countries, should find a way to be at unity in this?" (ed. Gardner D. Stout, Jr. [Berkeley and Los Angeles: University of California Press, 1967], p. 132).

18 Hartman, pp. 241-42.

19 Lindenberger, p. 241.

20 G. Wilson Knight, *The Starlit Dome* (Oxford: Oxford University Press, 1941), p. 81.

21 See, for example, Edward Ward, *St. Paul's Church; or, The Protes-*

tant Ambulators (London, 1716), a burlesque poem in praise of St. Paul's.

22 Cf. John T. Ogden, "The Power of Distance in Wordsworth's *Prelude*," *PMLA* 88 (1973):246–59.

23 John Strype, *A Survey of the Cities of London and Westminster . . .* (London, 1720), III, 240. See also Ward, *The London Spy*, I, x, 10.

24 *William Wordsworth's Literary Criticism*, ed. Paul M. Zall (Lincoln: University of Nebraska Press, 1960), p. 21.

25 Hartman, p. 239. See also Robert E. Park, "Community Organization and the Romantic Temper," in *The City*, ed. Robert E. Park, Ernest W. Burgess, and R. D. McKenzie (Chicago: University of Chicago Press, 1967).

26 C. C. Clarke, *Romantic Paradox: An Essay on the Poetry of Wordsworth* (New York: Barnes and Noble, 1963), p. 71.

Postscript

1 *The Poetry and Prose of William Blake*, ed. David V. Erdman, commentary by Harold Bloom (Garden City, N.Y.: Doubleday, 1965, slightly rev. 1970). All quotations of Blake's poetry are from this edition; parenthetical citations are to plate and line numbers. I follow the abbreviations of titles established by Erdman.

2 Raymond Williams, *The Country and the City*, pp. 148–49.

3 David Erdman, *Blake: Prophet against Empire*, rev. ed. (Garden City, N.Y.: Doubleday, 1969), p. 276.

4 For another discussion of this topic, see Kenneth R. Johnston, "Blake's Cities: Romantic Forms of Urban Renewal," in *Blake's Visionary Forms Dramatic*, ed. David V. Erdman and John E. Grant (Princeton: Princeton University Press, 1970).

5 Blake's letters are quoted from *Complete Writings*, ed. Geoffrey Keynes (London: Oxford University Press, 1966). Catherine Blake's phrase quoted above is found in her letter to Mrs. Flaxman, 14 September 1800.

6 Thomas R. Frosch, *The Awakening of Albion: The Renovation of the Body in the Poetry of William Blake* (Ithaca: Cornell University Press, 1974), p. 157.

7 I am indebted to S. Foster Damon, *A Blake Dictionary* (Providence, R.I.: Brown University Press, 1965), and to Stanley Gardner, *Blake* (New York: Arco Publishing Co., 1969), chap. 2, for information about Blake's London.

8 The explanation for Paddington's weeping is suggested by John

Beer, *Blake's Visionary Universe* (Manchester: Manchester University Press, 1969), p. 361.

9 In Erdman and Bloom, p. 847.

10 Erdman and Bloom, p. 847. My next sentence refers to Northrop Frye's essay, "Towards Defining an Age of Sensibility," in *Fables of Identity,* pp. 130–37.

11 Hartman, p. 309.

12 Quoted in Mary Moorman, *William Wordsworth: The Later Years, 1803–1850* (Oxford: Oxford University Press, 1965), p. 125.

Index